Radical Information Literacy

CHANDOS
INFORMATION PROFESSIONAL SERIES

Series Editor: Ruth Rikowski
(email: Rikowskigr@aol.com)

Chandos' new series of books is aimed at the busy information professional. They have been specially commissioned to provide the reader with an authoritative view of current thinking. They are designed to provide easy-to-read and (most importantly) practical coverage of topics that are of interest to librarians and other information professionals. If you would like a full listing of current and forthcoming titles, please visit www.chandospublishing.com.

New authors: we are always pleased to receive ideas for new titles; if you would like to write a book for Chandos, please contact Dr Glyn Jones on g.jones.2@elsevier.com or telephone +44 (0) 1865 843000.

Radical Information Literacy

Reclaiming the Political Heart
of the IL Movement

ANDREW WHITWORTH

AMSTERDAM • BOSTON • CAMBRIDGE • HEIDELBERG • LONDON
NEW YORK • OXFORD • PARIS • SAN DIEGO
SAN FRANCISCO • SINGAPORE • SYDNEY • TOKYO

ELSEVIER   Chandos Publishing is an imprint of Elsevier

CHANDOS
PUBLISHING

Chandos Publishing
Elsevier Limited
The Boulevard
Langford Lane
Kidlington
Oxford OX5 1GB
UK
store.elsevier.com/Chandos-Publishing-/IMP_207/

Chandos Publishing is an imprint of Elsevier Limited

Tel: +44 (0) 1865 843000
Fax: +44 (0) 1865 843010
store.elsevier.com

First published in 2014

ISBN: 978-1-84334-748-4 (print)
ISBN: 978-1-78063-429-6 (online)

Library of Congress Control Number: 2014938140

British Library Cataloguing-in-Publication Data.
A catalogue record for this book is available from the British Library.

Typeset by Domex e-Data Pvt. Ltd., India

Contents

List of tables

About the author

Andrew Whitworth is Senior Lecturer in the School of Environment, Education and Development at the University of Manchester, UK. He is Programme Director of the MA: Digital Technologies, Communication and Education, which in 2012 was the winner of a Blackboard Catalyst award for innovative communications strategies. He has been keynote speaker at several international information literacy conferences including "Creating Knowledge VI" in Bergen, Norway, in 2010, "Information Literacy: a way of life?" in Denmark in 2011, and the UNESCO/IFLA conference on Media and Information Literacy in Moscow in 2012, at which he was also one of the authors of the UNESCO Declaration on Media and Information Literacy.

When not working he prefers to be found up a mountain somewhere, usually in the English Lake District. In his previous book, *Information Obesity* (2009, also published by Chandos), he was scolded by a reviewer for mentioning too often in the main text that he lives in Hebden Bridge, Yorkshire, and supports Brighton and Hove Albion FC. So he hasn't mentioned either fact in this book. Well, apart from just then.

Introduction

This is a work of social, political and educational theory that critically explores, and then contests, the field of information literacy (IL), by attending to its relationship with power and authority, and how these shape the generation of knowledge. The central argument of the book is that, since its emergence in the 1970s, IL has constructed and then institutionalised itself around a *monologic* approach that stands in a fundamental tension with the *dialogic* nature of learning, knowledge-formation, and the use of language (Linell 2009). This argument is based on a more expansive view of IL than is typical, one that addresses issues of dialogue, discourse, power, and authority over information exchange, and that has, as its field of interest, the *collective* creation of knowledge. Individual literacy – facility with information – is at the root of this, but this is always manifested within technological, organisational, social and linguistic structures that already exist and which impose *cognitive authority* (Wilson 1983) over information. This authority often goes unscrutinised. This book will argue that institutionalised, monologic forms of IL do not permit scrutiny of cognitive authority, but only reinforce it in ways that ultimately weaken the quality of collective decision making and knowledge formation in communities, in organisations, and in society. Hence, the need for a 'radical information literacy': the application of principles of informed, direct democracy to the scrutiny of information exchange within organisations and communities. Radical IL does not attempt to annul authority, but nor does it simply reinforce what cognitive authority exists; rather, it explores ways to *more widely distribute authority over information practices.*

To develop and justify radical IL, attention must be given to how IL has so far been theorised. It is theory, not practice, that the IL literature is lacking (Lloyd 2013; Bruce 2013). IL is supported by theories developed elsewhere, but not yet synthesised into a theory that IL can call its own; a philosophy of not only IL but also information science (Tomic 2010). Presently, IL finds its principal theoretical bases in: library and information science (LIS), and the design of information systems (e.g. Zurkowski 1974; Saracevic 1975; Breivik and Gee 1989); sociocultural practice theory (e.g. Lloyd 2010b; Limberg, Sundin and Talja 2012); personal construct psychology (PCP) (Kuhlthau 1993); phenomenographic studies of education/phenomenographic pedagogy and variation theory (e.g. Bruce 1997; Bruce et al 2006; Edwards 2006), and finally, albeit less influentially, critical theory (e.g. Andersen 2006; Elmborg 2006; Whitworth 2007; 2009). This book reviews the contributions of each field to IL.

To this mix is then added Mikhail Bakhtin's theories of discourse. His theories permit a fuller exploration of the notion of *authority*. It is authority which pulls together the other theories, and the forms of IL derived from them. Ultimately, IL must attend to the ways in which cognitive authority becomes embedded in information systems, organisations, texts, and language itself. Through exploring the links between the various fields of IL mentioned above – particularly phenomenography and practice theory – this book describes how IL can help social actors discover in *practice*, and not just in theory, their own potential to democratically transform structures of authority over information exchange, and then maintain scrutiny over this authority.

* * *

Chapter 1 outlines the key concepts which will drive the argument, principally the notion of dialogism, and why this demands constant attention to *contexts*. It is in local contexts, or "information landscapes" (Lloyd 2010), that cognitive authority is determined by the various communities that reside within, and are constantly constructing, these landscapes. Chapter 2 then explores the origins of IL, and suggests that at these early stages, IL potentially had a sensitivity to literacy's political nature, and the role of information in both empowerment and disempowerment, that has since been lost. More precisely, it has been obscured by other, contemporaneous perspectives on the subject. Understanding why the political heart of IL was lost reveals biases in the systems used to organise the production and consumption of information in society, including the educational system. These systems are based on a particular notion of authority; that it is centralised, exclusionary and unitary, instead of distributed, participatory and polyvocal (many-voiced). These alternative forms of authority provoke not only the need for individuals and groups to *learn* about the patterns of information exchange and cognitive authority within their landscapes, but also how to *transform* these and *maintain vigilance* over authority. The seed of such an alternative view of IL is visible in a paper by Hamelink (1976), but its potential is undeveloped.

Chapters 3 and 4 investigate how IL did develop, both as a field of academic study and in practice. These chapters offer a brief political history of IL, with particular attention to the contributions of LIS, PCP, and phenomenography. The latter offers a very well-developed view of IL as *learning* – that is, something which changes the way we become aware of and experience our world. But most IL is taught, practiced and studied in limited ways, and chapter 4 presents evidence for the *institutionalisation of a monologic view of the subject*. Institutionalisation is a key contributor to the lack of scrutiny of cognitive authority: thus, it is opposed to direct democratic practice. Therefore, this institutionalisation, and its consequences for practice, must be specifically addressed by a radical IL.

Chapter 4 also notes that the most well-developed architecture, not only for *understanding* the contexts within which people experience information, but also for *transforming* these contexts, comes from those applying practice theory to work in IL. These authors include Lloyd, particularly her work on *information landscapes* (Lloyd 2010), and others, largely based in Scandinavia (e.g. Limberg et al 2012; Tuominen et al 2005; Sundin 2008). However, institutionalised forms of IL have not been fundamentally challenged by this approach. I argue that this is in part because there is currently no full, theoretical integration of the practice-based view with the phenomenographic, *educational* view – one that recognises the fundamentally dialogic and political nature of knowledge formation in society.

The second part of the book (chapters 5–8) is therefore devoted to this task of integration. Chapters 5 and 6 explore the political and linguistic theories which are the foundation of the dialogic view of IL, first through assessing (but ultimately rejecting) the contribution of Jürgen Habermas to the field (chapter 5), then, in chapter 6, considering the work of Mikhail Bakhtin. This is an original application of Bakhtin, whose work has not yet featured significantly in discussions of IL, despite a shared interest in *dialogue*. Chapter 6 explores these theories and draws out from them the notion of authority, and eventually, an intersubjective view of IL that stresses the necessary *democratic transformation of information landscapes as an outcome of IL.* The key methodological connection (explored in chapter 7) between the phenomenographic and practice-based traditions lies in the way variation in perceptions of the information landscape are accommodated. This reveals the role of authority in the genesis and ongoing transformation of context-specific information landscapes, and how these landscapes can be seen as an outcome of learning.

Finally, chapter 8 returns to the idea that a radical IL would enhance actors' ability to perceive, scrutinize, and transform the structures of authority over information exchange and, based on the preceding theoretical synthesis, explores what work has already been undertaken in this area and proposes agendas for both research and practice in radical IL.

* * *

This book is a critical theory of education, but it is one that specifically challenges notions that education is something limited to formalised institutions. The book is intended for all practitioners of IL, wherever they may be located: in libraries, in schools, in community organisations, activist groups, or businesses. In their detailed and influential exploration of educational theory, Carr and Kemmis (1986, 41) state that: "the development of a critical theory of education must be related intrinsically to the professional development of teachers." While radical IL is certainly educational, however, it is key to the argument of this book that it be viewed as relevant to all educational processes in society, including, but going well beyond, formal education such as that practiced in schools or colleges. The ways we view the role of the 'teacher' – and how these different views impact, in turn, on approaches to teachers developing their competencies, and helping learners to do the same – are integrated into the structures through which authority and institutionalisation are sustained. Exploring in a broader sense what it means 'to teach information literacy' allows this book to make contributions to the social and political theories of communication and knowledge-formation, and to explore how this takes place not only in the formal arena of the classroom, with its relatively prescribed structure and close monitoring by various high-level agencies, but in many other arenas including workplaces, the family, the media, and social networks.

The book takes an exploratory approach to IL, rather than an evaluative one (Lundh, Limberg and Lloyd 2013). That is, it does not accept one or more definitions of IL as givens, or standards, then discuss how educators can design and evaluate programmes of teaching to help improve learners' progress towards these standards. Nor, however, does it ignore these programmes and the standards on which they are based. Standards are evidence of a monologic approach to IL, but that means they must be engaged with, not ignored or dismissed as inappropriate. IL standards are evidence of the role of cognitive authority and power in IL; but like all such authorities, they can be turned into *positive* resources for learning *if* subjected to scrutiny by those working with the standards. Only through taking this view is there a chance that IL's theory-practice gap can be closed.

For similar reasons, the book also turns a critical eye on the role of the library in IL. As chapter 4 will show, the institutionalisation of IL in the library is an actively damaging phenomenon. But to effectively challenge the isolation of IL in the library – a call to arms made frequently by librarians writing on the subject (e.g. Badke 2012; Secker and Coonan 2013) – one must also investigate why it exists; that is, what the isolation is evidence of. This cannot be done solely within the bounds of LIS. The theories that this book draws on most heavily are not, with one exception (Kuhlthau's work, described in chapter 3), theories of librarianship. Nor is radical IL a 'library practice', although it may be undertaken in a library, by librarians. Nevertheless, as the book seeks to inspire the transformation of practice, there are points at which it directly addresses library practitioners. The book is a critique of the library's dominant role in IL, albeit one that offers at least some tools that practitioners can use to understand and change this role from within. Beyond the library, the book should also be useful for anyone interested in theories of information, information behaviour, and workplace learning, whether or not they are members of the LIS profession or other disciplines.

The development of a radical IL must also be technology-independent. The emergence and present ubiquity of information and communications technologies (ICTs) are clearly significant influences within the information landscapes of society, and critical views of ICT's potentially negative impact on learning have long been advanced (e.g. Roszak 1986; Robins and Webster 1987). ICT, rather than innately being a tool for autonomous learning and personal enlightenment, may be more accurately identified as part of the structure by which the powerful in society maintain their *capital*. In *Information Obesity* (Whitworth 2009) I reviewed the history of ICT in education using the same broad critical theoretical background as used in this book. This time, however, ICT's role is tangential. The arguments herein draw on theories of learning, practice, and democracy as they play out in an environment in which there is rapid technological change, but which are not driven by these changes except insofar as they provoke learning needs which must then be solved. I will go so far at this point to state that if the notion of *'information literacy'* is to have any hope of acquiring an independent theoretical base, it must be a technologically-neutral theory.

What this book is, ultimately, is a methodology: an exploration and evaluation of a set of *cognitive* tools, provided by other authors but synthesised here into a framework by which we (meaning, participants in real discourses) can learn to see the potential for transforming systems of informational exchange into more democratic forms, and thus more widely distributing cognitive authority.

* * *

I must gratefully acknowledge the friends, colleagues and institutions who helped me write this book. Most of the work was done between January and August 2013, thanks to a sabbatical from the Manchester Institute of Education at the University of Manchester, UK. There, I thank Helen Gunter, Julian Williams and my colleagues on the MA: Digital Technologies, Communication and Education (Gary Motteram, Susan Brown, Alan Jervis, Mike O'Donoghue, and Marilena Aspioti). My students on the *Media and Information Literacy* course unit have patiently helped me explore these ideas over the years: this book is the culmination of that process so far, but not, I hope, its end. Stephen Pearson of the University of Manchester Library undertook a literature search for me and I thank him for his time and attention to a task that proved invaluable, considering my "shabby skills" (Badke 2011, 133) in this area. At this European end of operations, Fred Garnett, Susie Andretta, Anna Hampson Lundh, Geoff Walton, Anne Kakkonen, Maria Carme Torras i Calvo, Ricardo Blaug, and A. Wainwright have also helped, in various ways.

My sabbatical was spent largely in Australia, courtesy of an invitation from the Queensland University of Technology (QUT), where I must thank Christine Bruce, Helen Partridge, Christine Yates, Ellie Abdi, Deb Ponting, Michael Rosemann and, for smoothing my stay in Brisbane, Fiona Doyle, Manuela Leemann, Debi Waters, and Wendy and Chris at the Kookaburra Inn, Spring Hill. Outside QUT I must also give thanks to Annemaree Lloyd, Bhuva Narayan, Stephen Kemmis, Caroline Bailey, Sharon Edwards, and Michael and Sharon Wray – not to mention Joy Division, Jello Biafra, Led Zeppelin, LCD Soundsystem, Neil Young, and sundry others – for all contributing in different ways to my personal information landscape and the inspiration I could draw from it over those months in the Southern Hemisphere. And a 'stop press' thank you to Peter Leigh, who helped recover the digital version of the manuscript of this book when my MacBook Pro's hard disk failed literally the day before I was due to submit it to the publisher in December 2013.

Finally, there would be no point to any of it without Clare and Joe, who put up with my foibles and absences well beyond the call of duty, and my families and friends in the UK who probably wonder why, but help anyway. Thank you to everyone; a big, deep-down thank you.

Part 1:
Deconstructing IL

"I need some information!"

"Sam, this is information retrieval, not information dispersal."

Sam (Jonathan Pryce) and Jack (Michael Palin) in *Brazil*
[dir: Terry Gilliam]

1

Basic concepts and terminology

Abstract: This chapter introduces key concepts and clarifies terminology, setting the scene for the discussions of IL which follow. It presents information as a specifically human property, one that links the subjective and personal, and intersubjective, collective realms. It explores the nature of dialogic and monologic approaches to meaning-making, recognises the importance of context and the existence of inequalities and irregularities in information landscapes. It discusses the role played in information exchange by creations such as artifacts, organisations, and communities, and the different ways these embody dialogic and monologic forms of thinking.

Key Words: Dialogism, monologism, intersubjectivity, context, information landscapes, artifacts, communities, cognitive authority.

This book, like all academic works, adopts a particular perspective on its subject. It takes a specifically sociopolitical view of IL, being concerned with relationships and dialogues between conscious human beings who act within the world and transform the world as a result. 'Information' is a concept with diverse definitions (Bawden 2001; Cover and Thomas 2012) and it is possible to view information purely technically, as a mere property, transmitted via a network or system. This technical view therefore also considers information a property of biological systems, even of the universe as a whole. To study information *literacy*, however, it is necessary to focus on information as a human property. Information can be generated through some kind of interaction with non-human environmental elements, but most is generated through interactions with other people, within a variety of contexts. It is by contextualising, through active cognitive work at a particular place and time, that raw data becomes information and, in turn, develops into knowledge. Information, knowledge, and communication are enmeshed with one another. Thus, information is essential for learning, and the consequent transformation of the world.

Interpretations of the world are necessary in order to interact with it, and these interpretations originate with *cognition*. Linell (2009, 14) defines cognition as: "intelligent or non-random coping with the world (in perception, thinking, acting and preparing to act etc.)". It involves interaction with the world, though not always with people at each and every moment. In this process, it is not information processing that is central, but *meaning* (Linell 2009, 221); cognition is therefore the *making of meaning or sense*.

Yet to consider human cognition as solely an individual, and thus essentially biological, property is a fallacy. For a start, it is difficult to deny the notion of an "extended mind" (*ibid*, 146–7), seeing cognition as dependent on not only the human brain but various tools, props, artifacts, texts and technologies. The enhancement of human cognition, through the ever-improving design of supplements like these, is the basic driver of information science. And, once one looks beyond the individual human brain and its biochemical operations as the sole basis of cognition, one is also forced to acknowledge that 'mind' (as opposed to 'brain') is a *relational* phenomenon. The human mind is a point of interaction – of *dialogue* – between various systems (Linell 2009, 147). In monologic views of cognition (*ibid*, 45): "There is no active role for recipients. They only have to understand, that is... retrieve and reconstruct the sender's intentions." 'Literacy' in this perspective can be seen as those cognitive processes, in the recipient, which ensure the message is received as the sender intended. But the dialogic view sees meaning as constructed during communication, rather than existing prior to the communication (*ibid*, 38). That is, messages or *utterances* (Linell 2009, 238–9; Bakhtin 1986; chapter 6 below) "do not 'contain' meaning... but they prompt people to make meaning" (Linell 2009, 224).

The dialogic view of communication therefore posits that knowledge formation is not subjective (that is, a matter of information absorption and cognition at the personal level), but *intersubjective*, created between people who draw on and transform informational resources from the world as they do so. Indeed, it is this ongoing use and transformation of resources in which intersubjective knowledge formation can be viewed as residing. The idea of a collective mind, or 'noösphere', does not have to be a mystical phenomenon (cf. Teilhard de Chardin 1959, Misztal 2003). Instead, the noösphere, though intangible, is real and continually constructed by the activities of the thinking organisms (people) and the environments that it penetrates (Samson and Pitt 1999; Whitworth 2009, 3–10). Just as the process of biological reproduction works to sustain and evolve the biosphere, so the processes of communication sustain and evolve the noösphere. As Linell (2009, 361) says:

> The dialogical stance... does not posit an abstract, spiritual or Cartesian mental world; on the contrary, it insists that meanings cannot occur unless there are human beings with their bodies, brains and minds acting in the external world. This holds... to cognitive processes in thinking, imaging etc., which are distributed over brain, body and world.

Thus, the world of information is not some mystical 'out-there' phenomenon. It is created by us, exists within us, but is also encoded into the *tangible* world in bodies, acts, texts, technologies and social relations. Knowledge is *intentional* (Linell 2009, 241): "never disinterested; rather, it is always the product of particular groups of people who find themselves in specific circumstances in which they are engaged in definite projects." And knowledge is "dependent on communication between individuals for its genesis, evolution and maintenance, and for its disappearance; knowledge wilts away if it is never communicatively sustained across generations" (*ibid*).

* * *

Intersubjectivity allows for the distribution of knowledge, but this distribution is not necessarily smooth. Knowledge can be "unequally accessed by different people" (Linell 2009, 82). This inequality can arise for many reasons including differences in status, literacy, familiarity with a context, and so on, and revealing the nature of such inequality is the fundamental purpose of this book, and of radical IL. However, at this stage, this 'lumpy' distribution can be considered in a more abstract way; as the fundamental characteristic of the noösphere, and the basis of the ideas to be explored in this section: that is, *context* and the *information landscape*.

As Calhoun (1992, 37) says, the noösphere is: "a field of discursive connections.... In nearly any imaginable case there will be clusters of relatively greater density of communication within the looser overall field..." In the most general sense possible, these clusters are the various contexts in which every one of us exists and from which we draw the resources we need in order to engage in activity and practice. Dialogism "implies a thoroughly *contextual* theory of sense-making" (Linell 2009, 361), and Linell (*ibid*, 16) draws a further distinction between *realised contexts*, that is, those aspects, or resources, made "communicatively relevant by participants in situ", and *contextual resources*, that is, "various meaningful phenomena which are (in one sense or another) accessible and could potentially be made relevant". Both realised contexts and contextual resources include concrete situations, observations and perceptions of these, texts, background knowledge, artifacts, and social representations all of which contain "potentialities to evoke particular types of discourses, actions, attitudes etc." (*ibid*, 242).

Lloyd (2010, 2) describes *information landscapes* as "the communicative spaces that are created by people who co-participate in a field of practice", and it is this metaphor which will be adopted in this book to name the various contexts within which these practices occur, whether they are located in a workplace (as Lloyd tends to use the term), in a university, school, or among friends and family. Because the noösphere and information are intangible, we are almost obliged to use metaphors to describe it: indeed, these metaphors are "really almost our basic vocabulary for talk about thinking and learning" (Wilson 1983, 3). Yet the idea of a 'landscape' remains a productive analogy for thinking about how to describe information in context. All tangible, geographical landscapes are comprised of the same basic elements (water, rock, life), but the number of possible combinations and forms of these elements give rise to their incredible diversity: each landscape is essentially unique. However, general forms (mountain landscapes, deserts) still exist and can be described. Landscapes are also shaped by activity at the micro-scale, iterated again and again to bring about large-scale transformations over longer periods of time. All these things are equally true of information landscapes. The landscape is also something one *experiences* and *explores*, an engagement which "allows [one]... to map the landscape, constructing an understanding of how it is shaped" (Lloyd 2010, 2). Exploring, and mapping, an information landscape "requires the act of becoming informed"; that is, to form an idea about the relevant resources within the landscape and "to understand and make judgments about these activities in the context of what is considered acceptable practice by others who share the same contextual space" (*ibid*). From this it can be stated that (*ibid*):

> (T)he process of becoming information literate requires the whole person to be aware of themselves within the world... to experience information through the opportunities that are

furnished by the landscape or context; to recognise these experiences as contributing to learning; and, to take into account how the context and its sanctioned practices, sayings and doings enable and constrain information use.

The information landscape does not represent the totality of human existence: we still engage with the world at an even more fundamental level of bodily need and visceral experience. But it can be argued that anything with informative potential is part of the landscape, including not just textual information but other people (and their own bodily needs and experiences) and created artifacts and tools. These two particular ideas need more exploration.

The notion of 'community' is important for the argument developed here, and that term is used in preference to 'group', which, though it refers to a collective, does not capture the idea of *connections* between members in the same way. A community may be defined in many ways: as people who live in a particular village, neighbourhood, city or other geographical location; as the worshippers of a particular religion; followers of a particular sports team (Whitworth 2009, 17–18); colleagues in a workplace, with shared learning needs (a community of practice (Wenger 1998)); learners on the same course; even sufferers from the same disease. The common factor is that, within communities, things are shared. People are not members of the same local community simply because they live in the same town, but because of shared perceptions, a common view of issues (Clarke 1996, p. 24):

> A community is a set of shared relations understood internally more than it is a set of objective behaviours. In a significant sense it resides in the imaginations of the members of that community. In building a shared identity a community comes to have a set of shared intentions and dispositions about its past, its general account of its origins, of its place in the cosmos, of paradigmatic figures and personages that come to represent significant perceptions of its history and events that mark significant moments in its shared memory...

This does not imply consensus, for example that members of a community all share political views. It does, however, mean that community members, as well as drawing on their own subjective perspective, make judgments with reference to a "collective matrix of interpretation" (Wellmer 1991, 197) that arises within a particular information landscape, the creation of which has been a joint effort. At the same time, social and collective needs are influenced by individual needs (Maceviciute 2006). Thus, subjectivity and intersubjectivity are closely related, and individual cognition has a profoundly intersubjective character (Fleck 1935, 42 quoted in Douglas 1986, 12): "Cognition is the most socially-conditioned activity of man [sic], and knowledge is the paramount social creation".

These communities or "thought collectives" (Fleck 1935), can take diverse forms. Some are "transient and accidental" (Douglas 1986, 12), but some are stable and disciplined, infrastructures for the perpetuation of certain values, such as churches, trade unions, and political parties. This is why the notion of a 'collective memory' requires no mysticism to explain. Collective memories are stored in landscapes, their communities, and the information-processing systems which infiltrate them.

There is no need to idealise the community. Some communities may foster trust, but others are dysfunctional (Douglas 1986, 25). One might be considered a member of a community *by others* even if one does not accept the label, or the community interpretation of a situation. Rose (1996, 334) writes that sometimes "our allegiance to... communities is something that we have to be made aware of, requiring the work of educators, campaigns, activists, manipulators of symbols, narratives and identifications". Communities can be exclusionary, even totalitarian (the cult, say). They can be, not the opposite of governance, an arena in which self-empowerment can be permitted to flourish, but the *means* of governance (Rose 1996, 335). Communities can also prevent knowledge formation. Špiranec and Zorica (2010, 149) claim that the Web 2.0 era has allowed a proliferation of learning communities, "characterized by intense activities of knowledge acquisition, information use and sharing". Yet this proliferation is also criticised by Shenk (1997) as contributing to a fragmentation of understanding, with tools such as 'intelligent' search engines and social media encouraging us to draw on only the views of a phenomenon with which we already agree.

On the other hand, the notion of 'community' is highly fluid. A community is not a firmly-drawn zone, just as its information landscape is not. Communities and landscapes are diffuse, their boundaries unclear, just as a physical landscape may suddenly change but may also have wide zones of transition, visible at different scales from micro to macro. Most people are part of many communities, and can thus draw on a range of collective matrices of interpretation. Some individuals straddle boundaries, acting, transiently or more permanently, as brokers or crossing points between these matrices (cf. Star 1989), but others may keep their membership of particular communities quite separate from others, even secret.

Either way, communities and their intersubjective matrices of interpretation are, clearly, essential tools for the making of judgments about information and the development of practice. Yet their fundamental importance means their influence is often invisible and unarticulated: "The power of socially approved knowledge is so extended that what the whole in-group approves – ways of thinking and acting, such as mores, folkways, habits – is simply taken for granted... although the source of such knowledge remains entirely hidden in its anonymity" (Schutz 1964, 133).

* * *

The role of artifacts in the information landscape also needs exploration. Artifacts are constituent parts of information landscapes, but they are produced in different ways from the community, with its basis in dialogue.

Practical knowledge has always been embedded into artifacts (Burkitt 1999, 38–9). As noted above, cognition is distributed through brain, body, and world, and in every case artifacts play a mediating role. Artifacts are the product of cognition and collaboration, and through interaction with them, further insights are formed. The artifact has "replaced the gene as the mode of transmission and change within societies" (Burkitt 1999, 41; see also: Limberg et al 2012, 104*ff*; Vygotsky 1978; Engeström, Miettinen and Punamäki 1999). Not all artifacts are technological: a particular way of thinking, or the result of a process of intellectual inquiry, may also be encoded into a cognitive artifact such as a methodology, a set of standards, or the definition of a particular word, given form as an artifact by being encoded in a dictionary. Even insights and experiences which may stem directly from emotions, personal observations, epiphanies, and so on still need to be filtered through the artifacts of a given information landscape before they can be meaningfully expressed. Therefore (Limberg et al 2012, 106): "Information is not viewed dualistically as either placed within an individual or within an artifact; instead information and the meaning of information is seen as shaped through dialogue with artifacts in practices."

Burkitt links this with Gibson's (1979) idea of *affordance*. Affordances are properties that are not innate to an artifact, but are instead social constructs, assigned even to artifacts that occur 'naturally' in the environment (Burkitt 1999, 36). An example of the latter would be the way the affordances of a tree could lead to it being perceived as something to climb, something to photograph, something to use as shelter in hot or rainy weather, something that is in the way and should be cut down, or something to burn. Affordance is related to a slew of factors including the physical appearance or design of an artifact, but also the user's prior (subjective) experiences with a particular artifact, or type of artifact, and the intersubjectively agreed-upon, negotiated meanings that have developed around the artifact[1]. Thus, the artifact is a crystallisation of prior activities that have used that artifact, and "our way of 'being-in-the-world', of acting, knowing and thinking, is largely dependent on artifacts and how they re-form embodiment" (Burkitt 1999, 36). Limberg et al (2012, 108) say that:

> Tools are not neutral to our activities, they are impregnated with perspectives, norms and values which mediate our understanding of the world (Wertsch 1998, 40). They make us do and see things in ways that we are not always conscious of. For information literacy education this implies that it is important to reveal and make explicit the perspectives, values and beliefs connected to specific tools for information seeking and how the application and understanding of these tools differ in different practices.

Yet the "perspectives, norms and values" with which tools are "impregnated" are often not available for scrutiny. This is because artifacts are not dialogic (Linell 2009, 421–2). They cannot speak and converse. Affordances are both social and technical, and one can see the former kind as based in dialogue and communication *about* the artifact; this kind of dialogue may also permit scrutiny of an artifact's technical affordances. Nevertheless, even if this takes place, one cannot converse *with* the artifact. One cannot persuade it to change the way it functions or processes information. Though artifacts can therefore be repurposed and reused in various different ways, they also have an element of 'built-in-ness'; they are, in essence, *congealed products of earlier dialogues* (Bakhtin 1986, 185). The artifact is therefore a means by which dialogue transforms into monologue. Any given artifact has encoded within it a set of assumptions and perspectives on the world that may or may not have been *consciously* designed into it, but which have shaped it nonetheless, and the artifact will, in turn, mediate activity (Winner 1986; Williams and Edge 1996; Engestrom et al 1999).

The impact of modernity on human social relations has been most profoundly felt in the wide spread of artifacts that are no longer being developed by the communities they penetrate. Local, indigenous, and contextualised forms of knowledge are de-emphasised in favour of generic rules, 'best practices', and tools developed elsewhere and then imported into a particular context. The artifactual elements of the information landscape, around which practices form and which are shaped by these practices, are, due to industrialisation, no longer seen as something over which communities have ownership (Burkitt 1999, 136):

> With machine production and the rise of more sophisticated communications technology, people no longer felt that their own social being was embodied in the artifacts they produced. This is part of the experience Marx has referred to... as *alienation*... the artifact does not appear as the product of the social relations in which the person is involved, but as a sign of capital.

Empowerment within a particular information landscape is therefore, in part, a matter of how one retains control over the artifacts that mediate information exchanges within that landscape. These artifacts increasingly include ICT, hence the substantial overlaps between digital (or computer, ICT) literacy and information literacy (cf Wenger, White and Smith 2009), but are not limited to such technologies. It is precisely because artifacts are the congealed products of earlier dialogues that their role in a given information landscape – the relevance of a particular technology or procedure at a particular point in time – should be subject to ongoing scrutiny.

Making such a statement requires one to be cautious, however. It should not be argued that monologic knowledge, manifested in artifacts, is somehow a less desirable form of knowledge than dialogism. To do so would lead to a range of intellectual fallacies and pathologies, including relativism and counterknowledge, which Thompson's polemic (2008) defines as ways of thinking which may be (intersubjectively) agreed upon by many people, but which have no scientific validity. Astrology is a good (or bad) example: just because a great many people engage in dialogue about it does not root its claims in the same kind of knowledge as the claims of theoretical physicists about, essentially, the same subject matter (the influence of astronomical objects and forces on earthly, human life). Chapter 6 of this book will explore this critique in more detail, but it is important to prefigure it here as it also highlights the essential nature of both monologic and dialogic means of knowledge formation. Natural science deals with "voiceless things" (Linell 2009, 373), about which *authoritative* statements can be made by following particular methodologies; that is, knowledge-forming practices. Science does not use "special tricks of thinking, argument, proof or reasoning": "its methods of thought are simply refinements of common sense" (*ibid*, 84: via Conant 1951). Yet at the same time these are reliable methods: "Science has a territory in which it is without serious competition, it can show strong predictive and technological indications of competence, and it shows, over a wide range, a common front" (Wilson 1983, 85). Scientific statements, being informational resources, can subsequently form the basis of tangible artifacts, or technologies, that serve as a demonstration of the authority invested in the particular statement (Wilson 1983, 84–5). No working artifact has yet been constructed that is based on the principles of astrology: hence there are no grounds to accept it as valid *technical* knowledge. In essence, then, scientific inquiry is the prime means by which *cognitive authority* is asserted. The pronouncements of science are presented as if they have an authority that is not subjectively determined – a matter of opinion – but has *objective,* generalisable qualities.

In his seminal discussion, Wilson (*ibid*, 15) offers this basic definition of cognitive authority: "influence on one's thoughts that one would consciously recognize as proper". Although we engage with a wide range of informational resources as we make our way through life, our horizons – those elements of information landscapes that we are aware of and can engage with, at least potentially – remain unavoidably limited. Most of our knowledge comes to us not through direct experience, but at second hand, through meanings and concepts provided by others, via communications media. We recognise cognitive authority not only in individuals, but also in books, instruments and organisations (*ibid*, 81). Wilson's book is a detailed investigation of the question: among all these possible meanings and concepts, how do we make selections, and decide which, or whose, point of view to believe? In this *judgement* rests the assignation of cognitive authority, and it is a complex activity. Professional specialisation and the holding of an advanced degree in a subject are formal signs of cognitive authority that are recognised in a court of law (thus, permit a person seen as holding such authority to be called as an expert witness) – but the authority will only extend as far as the area of specialisation. Wilson describes how in everyday life we use many other techniques for judging authority.

Cognitive authority cannot be simply claimed, but nor can it be entirely reduced to some kind of objective principle, including scientific method (as there are disagreements about what constitutes valid method). Thus, assigning cognitive authority is always a fallible process, involving a variety of inquiries (formal, systematic or informal, casual) and also habits, deference to the authority of others, delegation of the cognitive work required and, inevitably, errors of judgement and/or deliberate ignorance.

Nevertheless, even if scientific inquiry is not the sole means of asserting cognitive authority, claiming a *primacy* for it seems self-evident. Yet it must also be remembered that while natural science cannot engage in dialogue with its objects of enquiry, it remains dialogic at the level of *analysis* (*ibid*). If it were not, it could not progress – any given investigation, or artifact, once completed and constructed, would represent the definitive view of its subject. This is clearly not the case. Scientists can and do disagree with one another; there are rival methods and schools of thought, and ongoing scrutiny of even the most fundamental postulates of natural science.

Such channels for critical attention are, *in principle*, built into the structures of scientific knowledge-formation within society. That is, the genre of science itself, and its various devices and characteristics, which include publication, peer review, presentation of one's methodology, open discussion at conferences, freedom of speech and reply, intellectual independence, and so on. Thus, though it is always necessary for knowledge formation to (monologically) assert some kind of position at the end of a process of inquiry (Linell 2009, 383), this remains only a "locally monological" position, and is embedded in a broader, dialogic environment, a tradition of logical sense-making (Linell 2009, 374). That is, any claims to objectivity remain open to *intersubjective* scrutiny (Carr and Kemmis 1986, 121–2):

> (S)cientific 'objectivity' is not something that can be secured by mechanically applying some logical proof or by appealing to a realm of uninterpreted neutral 'facts'. 'Objectivity' involves not a naive belief in neutrality so much as a shared intersubjective agreement about the sort of norms of enquiry and standards of rationality which will ensure that theories can be critically assessed without the undue intervention of subjective bias and personal prejudice... 'objective' reality is itself that which corresponds to the intersubjective agreement of a community of enquirers whose deliberations are

conducted in accordance with shared standards of rationality. 'Objectivity', therefore, is achieved when participants reveal a willingness to make their views and preconceptions available for critical inspection and to engage in discussion and argument that is open and impartial.

This last sentence provides an excellent definition of the notion of *scrutiny*. This kind of "critical inspection" is not a threat to the validity of science: in fact, it confirms it. The value – the *authority* – of science arises exactly because it permits such scrutiny of its own validity claims, through its methodologies and methods, and as a result requires the maintenance of "a critical community of enquirers which is open and pluralistic, where all are free to criticize the thinking of others and everyone can actively participate on equal terms" (Carr and Kemmis 1986, 122). And in order that such a community be sustainable, this attention must also be directed *towards itself*; that is, keeping its knowledge-formation processes under review, and, through dialogue, scrutinising them rather than reifying them. Thus, "it also requires an appreciation of the historical and social context within which questions arise and possibilities for action are shaped and regulated" (*ibid*). This process of review includes scholarly work and debate about methodologies and methods, but it also requires attention to the practices which shape this landscape.

Here, however, is where the apparently self-evident value of scientific knowledge-formation must be called into question. In the first place, while the methods described here are appropriate for understanding the 'voiceless' subjects of natural scientific enquiry, the human or social sciences are also dialogic at the level of their subject matter, as well as the level of analysis. Natural sciences deal with phenomena that are difficult or impossible to appreciate without some form of technical aid, either in terms of instrumentation, such as that necessary to observe processes at microscopic scales, or at a great distance, or by using cognitive tools such as mathematics. On the other hand, "[t]he business of the social sciences is everybody's business and not left by default to academic social scientists to investigate" (Wilson 1983, 89). The social sciences thus have far less compelling claims to cognitive authority than the natural sciences. It may be less "information literate" to go to one's spouse for information on the Higgs Boson rather than a scientific text[2], but few would say the same were one seeking advice on how to avoid a stressful situation at work. In the latter case, cognitive authority may be invested in a scientific investigation of the causes of stress – but the results of this investigation would still have to be applied in one's own context. In fact, it is through such application that the 'products' of social science are validated by their users. *Practice* therefore becomes the test of these insights in the way that *artifacts* are for more technical enquiries (Carr and Kemmis 1986; Wilson 1983). Yet practices, like artifacts, do not always remain 'owned' by the communities that engage with them, and for the same reason – that the resources available for knowledge formation are not uniformly distributed.

People can be actively excluded from participation in the discourse, denied access to the necessary spaces. Validity claims may be concealed. Harding (1993), building on Freeman (1984), points out how asserting that any discourse is free of these distortions in fact masks the distortions that remain. Carr and Kemmis, in the quotation above, warn against the dangers of a "naive neutrality", and thanks to writers like Kuhn (1970) and Goldacre (2008), few would now see all scientific texts as ideologically neutral and *innately* objective. But Harding would say that the "shared intersubjective agreement" which Carr and Kemmis then mention is an exclusionary one. For Harding, this exclusion is based on patriarchy, with male bias deeply hidden in the empiricist and positivist bias of most science, but she notes (1993, 50) that other social movements, concerned with addressing the failure of *knowledge-formation structures in society to meet their needs*, are also ill-served by these epistemologies. The ability to critically attend to the claims to objectivity is one largely restricted to other scientists. Thus, the scientific (and for Harding, patriarchal) establishment pulls toward it the necessary forms of enquiry, meaning and other features of the relevant information landscapes which can be used as resources; these are taken away from those 'outside' the professional boundaries who may wish to engage in critical scrutiny of the claims of those 'inside'. A classic case of this came after the 1980s Chernobyl nuclear disaster, when sheep farmers in Wales challenged governmental, science-based reactions to the problem of fallout that would have resulted in their flocks being killed. Instead, the farming community was able to present its own evidence to the contrary, that was eventually accepted (Wynne 1989).

"Every society, every epoch in human history is characterized by what it considers as legitimate knowledge, itself a historically contingent category. Therefore, every epoch has its own view on what counts as legitimate information sources" (Andersen 2006, 215). The resources needed to engage in the kind of enquiries which provide this legitimacy may be financial or technological; they may also be intellectual or linguistic. Access to these resources may be restricted in various ways. Cognitive authority may be based not on active scrutiny of claims, but on a lack of awareness of alternatives.

***

One cannot remove normative considerations from IL (see Lundh et al 2013) without risking counterknowledge and relativism – that is, the fallacy that a poisoner could be 'information literate' if they go about researching the manufacture of ricin in an approved manner, and then applying this knowledge to their desired end. An information literate person must understand the reasons why cognitive authority is invested in certain texts, people and methods, as well as related issues such as ethics and legalities. Nevertheless, cognitive authority (including that which resides in standards, ethics and laws) *can be* and *must be* challenged in certain circumstances. There is no way of defining what such circumstances will be in advance; instead, these are judgements made through dialogue and reflection in particular contexts. Thus, IL should be seen as the *scrutiny of claims to cognitive authority in particular contexts*.

It is far from inevitable that such scrutiny will take place at a given place and time. Wilson (1983, 21) points out that we rarely get the chance to conduct a direct test of knowledge and, in any case, would find this difficult unless we were already specialists (cognitive authorities) in the field. I may wonder about the values and assumptions which have gone into the word-processing software that I am using to write these words but, in practice, they are largely irrelevant and not preventing me from working, so I do not think about them. I may have a layperson's interest in physics and be interested in the consequences of the recent confirmation of the existence of the Higgs Boson, but I do not have the time to actively scrutinise the claims of the team who discovered it, nor of Prof Higgs himself. Most people do not take the time to investigate these kinds of matters, whether the subject matter is everyday or not. Time is limited, and we are predisposed to reduce the amount of cognitive work we must undertake in a given situation, falling back on established patterns, habits, routines and assumptions (Blaug 2007; 2010). Judgements about cognitive authority are made precisely because we delegate this kind of work, whether by consulting a textbook or asking a friend or associate (Wilson 1983, 139). We may also delegate authority more passively, by submitting to the *administrative* authority that is invested in an organisational hierarchy; in essence, letting an organisation do our thinking for us.

Organisations – whether formal (like a limited company) or informal (like a community) – affect the way we think and process information. These arguments, based principally on Blaug (2007), were written up in chapter 9 of *Information Obesity* (Whitworth 2009) and will not be repeated here in detail, but the key point was that organisations 'push' ways of thinking at their members, through *information systems*. The systems are *artifacts*, manifestations of particular ways of thinking (Blaug uses the term "cognitive schema" (Bartlett 1932)) that are more likely to originate from those in superior positions in the organisational hierarchy. In fact, these systems *constitute* the hierarchy, in every practical sense.

Different patterns of information exchange pertain in different contexts, just as do different patterns of economic exchange. In the latter case, Graeber (2012, ch. 5) notes that many economic exchanges at the micro-level are "communistic", based on reciprocity and not tallied, that is, not counting money owed and credited. He explains that while these exchanges operate frequently, particularly within groups of friends, families and other close communities, through human history they have become subservient to hierarchical, non-reciprocal patterns of exchange. Through these, *debts* are accrued, which Graeber identifies as the key driver of capitalism, war and other major historical events. There also exist pure exchange relations, which are accounted for by monetary transactions that may stem from debt, but which are not accompanied by obligations for the subordinate member, as they are in hierarchical relationships of exchange. Though these latter relations complicate matters somewhat, Graeber's basic opposition – reciprocal versus non- reciprocal/hierarchical exchanges – can also be used to classify information exchanges.

Although, as with any other worldly sphere (cf. Whitworth 2009, ch. 1), information landscapes exist at multiple scales and always contain elements (genres, practices) that do not conform to their general pattern, those which are more hierarchical have a greater concentration of authority within them than those which are more reciprocal. In a hierarchical information landscape, information tends to flow one way, towards those with power in the hierarchy. This information is typically gathered through audits, monitoring, 'reporting up', etc. Conversely, the deliberations and decisions of those at the top of the hierarchy are less frequently open to scrutiny from those below. These imbalances do not prevent those outside the hierarchy pushing information onto the power-holders, whether through voiced or published critique, protests of some kind, withdrawal of consent, etc. Sometimes this can be accommodated by power-holders by a Gramscian "passive revolution" (Gramsci 1971):

office holders may change; new practices may be designed at the system level and then imposed on the landscape. Through manipulation of meaning this may be displayed as yielding to pressure, but such changes have not *redistributed authority* within the information landscape.

Practical investigations of how authority can be distributed within a social setting have absorbed humanity for millennia, as this is the study of politics. From Pericles' *Funeral Oration* (see Blaug and Schwarzmantel 2001, 25–27), through Machiavelli's study of how the populace would always take better decisions than a monarch (*ibid*, 34–7), and into studies of small-group decision-making and how this can be facilitated (e.g. Gastil 1993), a great deal of guidance exists in this area even if, as Blaug noted (1999b), research and rhetoric in this area tends to ignore the small-scale, informal and context-specific practices which make up the bulk of political activity. What must be done from this point on is consider how IL and these practices can be integrated, to mutual benefit. Hierarchy is not an innately bad thing under all circumstances, but there is a need to remain *vigilant* over it, in order that its benefits can be maximised and its costs reduced. These costs include alienation, other social maladies, and environmental destruction, but the costs are also *cognitive*. They fall on communities and individuals in terms of reductions in their ability to learn, to process information effectively and avoid information obesity (Whitworth 2009), in the quality of resources available to communities, and in overt restrictions placed on their ability to access information, whether barriers are physical, linguistic or related to status and practice. Yet these negative effects are neither inevitable nor irreversible. Radical information literacy is the set of practices through which these challenges can not only be recognised, but actively countered.

This chapter has outlined the most significant concepts underlying this book: dialogism; context; information landscapes; communities; artifacts; cognitive authority, and scrutiny. What it has not really dealt with yet is *information literacy* itself, but that is the subject matter of the next three chapters.

Notes

1. See Sadler and Given (2007) for studies of the affordances of the information system that is the library.
2. Unless one happens to be married to a theoretical physicist.

The early days of IL

Abstract: This chapter examines how IL emerged as a theoretical and practical concept in the 1970s, with a particular focus on three papers: Zurkowski (1974), which is representative of the knowledge management approach to IL; Burchinal (1976), representative of the educational approach, and Hamelink (1976), representative of the transformational. It sees in Hamelink's paper the roots of a radical approach to IL, but one that has remained undeveloped.

Key Words: Origins of information literacy, information science, knowledge management, education, transformation, hegemony.

There are many definitions of information literacy. These definitions generally coalesce around the idea that IL is a set of "purposeful information practices" (Limberg et al 2012, 95). How these practices are understood varies greatly, depending on the theoretical perspective in use, even where that theory is not explicit (Limberg et al 2012). This diversity will be explored throughout the remainder of part 1, which is also the story of how certain IL definitions have become dominant.

I begin by revisiting three papers that appeared between the years 1974–76. These papers do not cover the entirety of IL's foundation as an empirical field, but are representative of three distinct traditions that developed from a point in history when, with the emergence of large databases, the impact of ICT on knowledge formation, patterns of work, and economic relationships was becoming visible. The papers discussed are by Zurkowski (1974), which is representative of the *knowledge management* approach to IL, Burchinal (1976), representative of the *educational* approach, and Hamelink (1976), representative of the *transformational*.

* * *

IL begins – or, at least, was first defined – within library and information science (LIS). This is by no means the only relevant theoretical tradition. As will be explained later, seeing IL as *only* the province of LIS is one problem with how the field conceptualises itself. But nevertheless the contributions of LIS to IL are significant, particularly in its early days.

Saracevic's history of relevance' is simultaneously a history of information science (1975[1]). He opens with this definition:

> Information science is a field and a subject that is concerned with problems arising in communication of knowledge in general and with records in such communication in particular, from both applied and basic points of view. It shares this concern with other fields, notably those... of librarianship and of documentation; thus, the sharing of concerns specifies the fundamental relationship between information science and librarianship...

Saracevic investigates how the search for relevance drives the development of information systems (applied information science). The ideal information system delivers 100% relevant information; exactly what the user wants, always. This is a complex design problem because of the context-dependent nature of relevance, its depending on both what is already known by the user, and what is generally known. From the 1940s, LIS addressed this problem via the principle that an information system is instantiated not only in its technical elements, but also its human ones. Thus, the development of information systems is a sociotechnical process (Luna-Reyes et al 2005). Partly this means that librarians, programmers, or other information professionals can be seen as components of the system, and thus, LIS is concerned with integrating the technical components of the system with its human ones most effectively. However, it also means that information *use* becomes a design factor. In systems like plumbing, why the user wants water, how the tap is turned on (how he/she 'phrases the query' for water) and what is done with the water are ultimately irrelevant to its effective delivery. In an information system this is not the case. The ability to access the product of an information system therefore depends not just on its functional operations, nor mere physical access to the system (Kuhlthau 1993, p. xvii):

> The objective of library and information services is to increase access to resources and information. Basic access is provided through selection, acquisition and organization of resources...

> Increased or enhanced access is provided primarily through two services, reference and instruction. Enhanced access encompasses intellectual as well as physical access. Physical access addresses the location of resources and information. Intellectual access addresses interpretation of information and ideas within resources.

LIS therefore has an interest in 'instruction', or user education: optimising use of the system, helping users shape requests in forms that can be effectively processed, and helping them make further judgements about relevance should the system provide too much information. In this concern lies the origins of IL, at least as it emerged from LIS.

Lancaster (1970, 56) is an early example of such work:

> The need for education of users of information services has been recognized for some time. In 1963 the President's Science Advisory Committee recommended that schools and colleges should develop programs to teach students how to retrieve and use published information. Unfortunately, very little appears to have been done along these lines either in the United States or abroad.... American universities, through schools of library and information science, are training information scientists and technologists but are doing very little to assist other departments of the university in producing research workers capable of exploiting the literature to fullest advantage.

Lancaster could have used the term 'information literacy', but did not. Instead this was first introduced in Zurkowski's 1974 position paper presented to the US National Commission on Libraries and Information Science. "Developing information literacy" is the first section heading. Zurkowski immediately notes that an "overabundance of information" – defined as the availability of information exceeding our capacity to handle it (cf. Whitworth 2009) – is a universal condition (Zurkowski 1974, 1). He takes an expansive view of what constitutes an information landscape, including all printed and computer-based media, and the skills necessary for the landscape to function and be sustained. Users are not a homogeneous group; instead (*ibid*, 2, emphasis in original): "The individual user has many facets and shows different needs to the information sources at different times for different purposes. *Anticipating these changing needs and packaging concepts and ideas to meet them is a major evolving economic activity*".

The emphasis displays the defining characteristic of Zurkowski's argument: its overt economic and political liberalism. Provision of quality information, and the resources needed to find and process it, are driven by the profit motive (*ibid*, 5): either directly (by providing information, organisations make a profit and raise taxes) or indirectly, as what he calls a healthy "Information Service Environment" is essential for the continued economic success of US industry. Zurkowski argues that hyper-competitiveness in information provision drives innovation, and there will be a market for any services that enhance users' control over information (*ibid*, 6).

Zurkowski then says (*ibid*):

> People trained in the application of information resources to their work can be called information literates. They have learned techniques and skills for utilizing the wide range of information tools as well as primary sources in molding information solutions to their problems.

He speculates (*ibid*, 7): "While the population of the US today is nearly 100% literate, only a small portion – perhaps one-sixth – could be characterized as information literates." He informally suggests that members of the "medical, governmental, business, sci/tech" professions are among that small proportion. This proportion should be increased, and "the work of the Commission should be viewed in terms of achieving total information literacy for the nation" (*ibid*, 8). For Zurkowski, the information economy already has the necessary "pluralistic" structure (*ibid*) and maximising its benefits should therefore be a policy priority. Information is not like air, a "free good" (*ibid*, 6); work in processing and understanding it is needed before it is usable information (*ibid*, 1). The capacity to undertake this work, using available resources in an optimal way, is therefore an essential aspect of the Information Service Environment. Spreading this capacity is what helps provide the intellectual, and also the political, support for the investment of financial resources (profit and taxes) the Environment represents.

The remainder of the paper develops, not the notion of IL (which from that point, Zurkowski mostly sidelines), but the nature of this Information Service Environment. Zurkowski explores the assumptions which underlay the "Reading Services Environment", the pre-digital information infrastructure. That environment, comprised of entities such as public libraries, educators, and private interests (including publishers, donors) was (*ibid*, 23):

(A) healthy, dynamic institutional framework for harnessing the nation's pluralistic resources to the task of creating a reading literate society and a competitive marketplace of ideas... Three major time tested policies contributed to the success of the Reading Service Environment and their application to the Information Service Environment is essential to its successful operation:

1) Individual fulfilment, the advancement of knowledge and the discovering of truth, participation in decision making by all members of society, and achieving an adaptable and stable community depends on a system of freedom of expression.

2) Govenment should not perform services for citizens which citizens are capable of performing for themselves.

3) Government has a legitimate responsibility for assuring educational opportunities for all.

But the rise of ICT has brought about changes in the balance of the Reading Services Environment, particularly between libraries and industry, who may now see themselves in a state of competition when it comes to information provision. Zurkowski's part II describes the emergence of "information banks"; large electronic databases, machine-readable files and so on, offered by several institutions including Standard and Poor's and the New York Times. Parts III and IV discuss the evolving relationship between libraries and industry, describing new products and markets that are opened up by the development of information banks and new media for storing and transmitting information.

Zurkowski suggests that to maintain the healthy pluralism of the Reading Service Environment, policy changes are required, that acknowledge how ICT shifts relationships between publishers, readers, libraries and information providers. This is the key passage (*ibid*, 23):

With the introduction of new information processing technologies the line between marketplace and subsidized functions in some respects has become blurred. The process of achieving information literacy involves defining that line clearly and realistically, and in defining an institutional framework for the Information Service Environment. In our age of information overabundance, being information literate means being able to find out what is known or knowable on any subject. The tools and techniques and the organizations providing them for doing that form this institutional framework.

These tools, according to Zurkowski, must be built around the three core principles of the Reading Service Environment, described earlier. But the Information Service Environment would only become accessible to those who had achieved information literacy. Therefore, at the end of his document Zurkowski reiterates the need for the Commission to establish a programme aimed at achieving "universal" IL within ten years, which he says will (p. 27):

> (I)nvolve the coordination and funding of a massive effort to train all citizens in the use of the information tools now available as well as those in the development and testing states.... Until the population as a whole is prepared to utilize and benefit across the board from the capabilities of the Information Service Environment, proposals to create systems serving the elite alone will lack the popular political support needed to obtain the level of government funding suggested in the Report of the Commission.

This review of Zurkowski's argument serves to highlight the assumptions which informed his early call for IL. His position is one of *economic pragmatism*, wholly situated within a US context. Zurkowski's liberalist stance holds that the US government's role should be to sustain free market competition. As informational resources are taking on forms which a minority of the population are currently equipped to handle, more information literates need to be produced, to sustain the nation's economic competitiveness and political liberalism. But beyond this, Zurkowski offers no view of *agency*. No particular mention is made of learning: "education" gets a section heading at the end (*ibid*, 27), but this is a short conclusion, quoted above almost in its entirety. There are no references to specific educational institutions, whether universities, schools or training companies, nor to pedagogy. In addition, Zurkowski's emphasis on "information banks" obscures the broader nature of information landscapes, and the recognition that IL skills can, and should, be applicable to stocks of information held outside such databases, in oral, embodied or cultural forms. And finally, Zurkowski makes no mention of the *individual's* ability to judge relevance, filter information, be aware of intellectual property and copyright, and so on, though these are all implied as properties of the information systems which are being developed.

This latter observation, viewed through the framework for analysis outlined in chapter 1 above, permits the conclusion that all the economic, even the political, benefits that Zurkowski sees as flowing from widespread "information literacy" could be secured by optimising the *non*-human elements of the information system. Mastering data mining tools, or an automated information filtering service, could count as "information literacy" by this definition. Therefore, there is a *depersonalising* element in Zurkowski's work, one that is already prefigured in LIS and exacerbated precisely by the emergence of giant information banks, resources which extend beyond the compass of single human consciousnesses and their immediate networks and communities. These issues of scale had emerged before; Vannevar Bush (1945), with the memex, for example, had offered a technical response. Zurkowski's work fits into this tradition, with IL a way of thinking that would optimise the human elements of information systems. His aim is to train people's imperfections away, through means specified by others. Arguably, what has developed from this particular seed is not IL at all, but information and knowledge management.

Yet, coupled with Zurkowski's economic liberalism there is his political liberalism, his emphasis on a plurality of voices and opinions, freedom of expression, and individuals' rights "not only... to speak, but also to be heard" (*ibid*, 25). These simultaneously give his appeal for IL a universalist character, positioning it as something which is fundamental not just to the health of an economy, but also to a political system and decision-making in society as a whole. The details may be absent but the higher-level position is clear: information literacy is for everyone, it is a fundamental aspect of communication, a shaper of possibilities. To repeat a quote given earlier (*ibid*, 23): "In our age of information overabundance, being information literate means being able to find out what is known or knowable on any subject. The tools and techniques and the organizations providing them for doing that form this institutional framework." The words "known *or knowable*" are essential. Information landscapes are dynamic, not static; what we will need to know in future situations is not predictable. Therefore, to sustain the liberal, politico-economic system, Zurkowski implies that the increased availability of information requires us to attend, at least, to the *way we shape knowledge* – and perhaps, to change how we do this, if old means of knowledge-formation (cognitive authorities) are no longer appropriate and/or the institutions which support these are no longer fit for purpose. Thus, Zurkowski offers IL more as an *epistemology* than a form of learning, a way of understanding how we can know what there is to know (Grix 2002). He believes it would be a means towards particular political and moral ends, or at least, contribute to an environment that made those ends more achievable.

* * *

The next seminal IL paper was a speech made by Lee Burchinal in 1976 at the Texas A & M library conference in 1976, the US's bicentennial year (hence its calling the communications revolution "America's Third Century Challenge"). It is worth highlighting next because, while it shares many concerns with Zurkowski's paper – the need to prepare for imminent changes in the informational environment, wrought by digital technologies – it ends with a more specific appeal to education as the realm in which IL could be nurtured. The speech has been little cited since, and even then, not always correctly. Pinto et al's recent (2013) reference calls it a contribution from "journalism", which is at best misleading. Burchinal was a sociologist at Iowa State, with many 1950s-60s publications on the family, marriage, and parenting. The reason he addressed the library conference was his role in developing ERIC, the Educational Research Information Center, which became one of "the world's most authoritative, computer-based, knowledge-exchange services" (Dentler 2002, 120), and an exemplar of an information bank.

Most of Burchinal's speech offered evidence for claims that the information industries had, by 1976, become the most significant sector of the US economy, larger than manufacturing, agriculture and services combined. Real costs of communication were dwindling, and bearing in mind this and other drivers, such as a need to conserve energy (Burchinal 1976, 10–11), Burchinal correctly anticipated a future in which more jobs and personal experience – banking, purchasing, communications with friends and work associates – would use terminals (*ibid*, 11). He acknowledged that some universities, in engineering, science, and business administration, had begun to instruct students in computer operations, and LIS instruction was also "in healthy ferment" (*ibid*). But more was necessary, he said, repeating Zurkowski's call to "set about systematically to create 'information literacy' for all adults in the nation, so each can function effectively in our emerging society" (*ibid*).

At this point Burchinal did two things differently from Zurkowski: he defined IL more precisely, and he suggested an institutional location for the work of creating IL. IL, he said (*ibid*, 11):

> (R)equires a new set of skills. These include how to efficiently and effectively locate and use information needed for problem-solving and decision-making. Such skills have wide applicability for occupational as well as personal activities. Part of such competency includes comfortable use of a computer terminal for sifting through available information from various data banks to select useful data for resolving the problem at hand.

Burchinal did therefore include digital literacy as a part of IL, but only a part. He defined it similarly to his contemporary Nevison (1976; see Whitworth 2009, 84–5), as the ability to use a computer, although with less of a focus on programming and more on information searching.

Whereas Zurkowski's argument was presented in libertarian terms, Burchinal used more instrumental language. The project to create IL should be "systematic", and IL itself was about "effectiveness" and "efficiency". Burchinal did not, even implicitly, call into doubt any aspect of the emerging information society (cf. Webster 2002); his argument was that it is upon us, and thus society has a responsibility to train everyone in the needed new skills. Specifically, this was an *educational* issue. Universities that did not address this would be damaging their graduates' prospects (*ibid*, 12), not only in occupational life, but in personal and home life too.

A significant passage followed (*ibid*): "As these technologies become more common, elementary schools will take over the responsibility for creating information literate citizens. Universities, however, can ill afford to wait. Also university experience, as in so many fields, can become the basis for subsequent school programs." Burchinal clearly saw universities' teaching of IL as a transitional stage. Universities might come to offer similar assistance as they do to primary and secondary teaching in other subjects (training teachers, researching pedagogy, offering advanced curricula), but the bulk of IL education should eventually take place in schools.

Taken as a whole, and looked at with nearly four decades' hindsight, Burchinal's speech offers little that seems exceptional. Had it not been cited in Behrens (1994) it may have been lost[2]. Nevertheless, it is an example of how IL began to sprout from the seed Zurkowski planted, and an early case study of IL trends that became dominant in the 1980s, particularly in the US (see below). With Burchinal, IL becomes identified as a specifically *educational* problem: how to develop in people the skills needed for the effective and efficient seeking of information, for problem-solving and decision-making. Therefore, though Burchinal, like Zurkowski, takes a high-level view, IL is presented as something more concrete than an epistemology. Not skills to establish what is knowable, but what is already known.

* * *

The third paper may represent the first use of the term 'IL' outside the US. The Dutch writer Cees Hamelink's "An Alternative to News" appeared in the *Journal of Communication* in 1976, and outlines a different form of IL. Hamelink retains Zurkowski's emphasis on freedom of expression, but with a stronger critique, through invoking Freire's view of literacy as the basis for IL. Hamelink does not see IL as a skill that must be acquired so a person can be fitted into a technology- and information-rich system that is currently being designed by others, but a more bottom-up, personal characteristic that allows this systematisation to be countered and critiqued. This view is made clear in the first sentence, typeset as a heading (1976, 120): "A new 'information literacy' is necessary for liberation from the oppressive effects of the institutionalized public media." Hamelink describes how individuals act within information landscapes that are pre-defined and filtered by dominant interests in society (*ibid*):

> (W)hat is actually communicated [in the public media] is the outcome of a decision between possible alternatives which is made on the basis of the most powerful interests (economic, hierarchical, intellectual).

Because these interests "select items for the public agenda" (*ibid*):

> "(I)nformation" functions as an oppressive tool since, by its manner of presentation, it keeps people from shaping their own world. The incoherent fragments preclude the wholistic perspective which enables insight into the interdependence between happenings, into the involvement of one's own context, and into the possibility of acting upon the challenge thus posed. The ready-made explanations preclude the insight of the world as something problematic and changeable.

These are crucial points. Zurkowski and Burchinal see IL as something that needs to be developed *in* populations in order to assimilate them into the emerging ICT- and information-rich society. Hamelink sees IL as something that has to be developed *by* populations so they can defend themselves against the *cognitive costs* of that society (*ibid*, 120–1):

> If, however, people are to be given the chance to intervene in their reality, then information channels have to be created that do permit the coherent organization of information.... [This] would require (a) the presentation of perspectives otherwise suppressed, (b) user orientation (in the sense of relating to genuine needs), (c) the generation of information (the sharing of insights).

Hamelink writes (*ibid*, 122) that "the first step toward 'information literacy' is to recognize that access to information starts from where the information users are". Therefore (*ibid*), "their situational context... is central". Information is not merely something to be given to people, or retrieved by them, but formed and then shared by them, as a response to people's felt needs and through their own efforts. This *dialogue* is how connections are made between "unrelated fragments" offered by the media (*ibid*).

Dialogue may develop within some kind of formal learning process, but as recognised by Freire (1970), such learning has to be sensitive to the needs, and political/social context, of the learners, and not something which has had its content and context determined by others, in a paternalistic way. When one population colonises or oppresses another, the very meaning of the term 'literacy' becomes skewed towards the texts and values of the coloniser, and imposed through the educational system. For example, examinations will be set in the dominant language, requiring it to be used in schools, where children study canonical texts (in book form) from the coloniser's culture and history rather than their own (where these narratives may exist only orally). These were common tendencies in Africa and South Asia throughout the 19th and 20th centuries, and for minority languages within developed countries (e.g. Catalan, Welsh). Freire's *political* literacy education involves not just instruction in the technical aspects of reading and writing, but *dialogue that raises awareness of the value of one's own culture, history, and associated information landscapes.*

Literacy education can thereby liberate and empower a population who are having their information landscapes shaped by interests that are not their own, and in fact are actively oppressing them. This directly informs Hamelink's view of IL. He goes into more detail than Zurkowski and Burchinal regarding how and where IL can be implemented, writing that (*ibid*, 123):

> (A) vital step towards 'information literacy' is the implementation of community centers which give access to a set of information resources with which the user can interact, i.e., ask for and receive information at his own initiative and in his own perceived self-interest. To avoid sophisticated forms of well-intended paternalism, such centers would have to be designed and developed with a major input from those who are supposed to benefit from them.

Zurkowski's notion of 'information banks' is thus turned on its head. The banks are now not giant databases; that is, specific *objects*, with technological features that shape interactions with the information, and require a certain type of organisation and management to be effective. Instead, the 'bank' is transmuted into a *location* in which a range of resources can be found that are specific to context and over which the user has some control. Within this environment (*ibid*), IL depends not just on offering people skills (though it does this in part), but also on raising awareness of *possibilities for transformation* (*ibid*), via discussion, debate and simulation:

> The process of becoming the object of one's history has to start with the awareness of the immediate context and the consciousness that this context is changeable.... The information search-and-find procedure would have to be complemented with the awareness of the meaning of new alternatives. Those who used these alternatives would need to become conscious of their creative potential... One important experience in this regard would be to create opportunities for the information-powerful and the information-powerless to reverse roles. Community decision-making would also have to be simulated to make visible what is at stake in terms of the power, interests, motives, and assumptions invested in these communication processes. Finally, situations should be simulated in which people can experience how far-reaching and powerful their information can be.

Through this work, informational resources are actively *shaped* by the users, in accordance with their needs, rather than just being a 'bank' from which withdrawals are made on the terms of those who control it (note the link with Freire's 'banking' model of education). Hamelink does not discount the role of the 'expert' in this shaping, making specific reference to the work of certain media organisations (*ibid*, 121). But he firmly recognises that such work cannot make others 'literate' on *their own* terms: literacy cannot be reduced to a set of generic capabilities or skills, but varies according to need and context. Hamelink's is therefore a firmly political definition of IL which recognises differences between people and interests, and presents IL as something which is oriented towards empowering the usually disempowered in society.

***

These are not the only three 1970s authors whose work could have been quoted here. Behrens (1994) cites contributions by Taylor (1979), who wrote specifically about librarianship and noted, among other things, the difference between a *continual* "informing process" and the on-the-spot "information [retrieval] process". Owens (1976, 27) wrote of IL as an essential element of democracy:

> (V)oters with information literacy are in a position to make more intelligent decisions than citizens who are information illiterates. The application of information resources to the process of decision-making to fulfill civic responsibilities is a vital necessity.

'Political' as this is, Owens still casts the information literate individual in much the same way as Burchinal and Zurkowski: as suffering from a skills deficit that, writ large, threatens the stability of existing institutions. The idea of democracy existing outside these institutions – and being central to the workings of communities and how they maintain their information landscapes – is not present in the same way as in Hamelink's paper.

What the three papers – Zurkowski, Burchinal and Hamelink – jointly reveal is a key theme of radical IL: that it is essential to see information as context-specific. Hamelink acknowledges – where Burchinal and Zurkowski do not – that the various contexts within which information is processed are not equal. They manifest different *ways of thinking and forms of cognitive authority*, and so, within them, information is *validated* differently. These differences are not simply technical characteristics, that can be allowed for in the design of an information system, but *political*, and result in practices and artifacts developed in one context being inappropriately applied in another, through the development of information systems that instantiate cognitive authority in particular ways. As a result, the information system in use becomes inappropriate for certain users, and the relevance of informational resources within the system for these users is reduced.

In that the previous sentence can be classed, more or less, as a statement of pure information science (cf Saracevic 1975), this shows that information systems and information literacy cannot be investigated without appreciating their political nature. The institutional location of IL, and the reasons why it is being called for and practiced in certain ways, are political questions.

Freire is the only person cited by Hamelink in this paper, but the work of another writer is clearly invoked, if not explicitly cited: Antonio Gramsci. Gramsci recognised that control within a society was not usually asserted by direct oppression and force, but rather through the channels of *hegemony*. Hegemony is (Gramsci 1971, 12):

1. The 'spontaneous' consent given by the great masses of the population to the general direction imposed on social life by the dominant fundamental group; this consent is 'historically' caused by the prestige (and consequent confidence) which the dominant group enjoys because of its position and function in the world of production.
2. The apparatus of state coercive power which 'legally' enforces discipline on those groups who do not 'consent' either actively or passively.

Hegemony does not require the use of force. If the state needs to use force to maintain itself, asserted through an army or police, then it has lost its hegemony (*ibid*). Rather, consent to the existing order is manipulated through the control of societal elements such as law, education, political parties, the media, and language. These channels are used to deflect the impact of crises (for example, economic recessions) away from the ruling classes that cause them (Adamson 1980, 11).

Hegemony is not totalitarian. The media which sustain it are all potentially available to a *counterhegemony*, a necessary part of any political transformation (Holub 1992, 91). Transformation needs to occur in multiple arenas (economic, cultural, sociological, linguistic, etc), and is not a single 'rupture' between old and new. Such revolutionary moments can be defused by a dominant group using the channels of hegemony (Adamson 1980, 225). Instead, a counterhegemony creates conditions in which alternatives can flourish: communicative spaces, values, practices, and forms of cognitive authority that collectively change the resources available to groups and communities (Simon 1991, 29). Hegemony is not a fixed condition, but a *communicative process*, which must constantly update itself, reacting to ongoing events, if it is to remain uncoercive (Urbinati 1998). To justify itself without coercion, an elite must open up, for public display and scrutiny, certain claims on which its position is based. This will produce a range of discourses, which may be in contradiction with one another. These claims become *resources* available for exploitation, particularly if they do not accord with the subjective experience of those subject to elite rule (Scott 1990: see also chapter 6 below). Critiques of any political system which base themselves on contradictions in the validity claims of elites are legitimate critiques by definition (Scott 1990, 106). Thus, change is inherent in the uncertainties of language and the shifting nature of the claims used by the powerful to validate their position: no discourse can ever represent the totality of social life (Melucci 1996, 212–3). And though (Holub 1992, 115–6):

> (L)anguage, in its form as a structure of values, and mediated by agents of the hegemonic class, can keep the subaltern social classes in check... subaltern classes can invent new structures of value designed to subvert this hegemonic design... For Gramsci, this invention of counterhegemonies is in part contingent of the very structure of language itself.

Because education is one of the conduits of hegemony – a means through which the hierarchical and inegalitarian structures of a society can be presented as natural and normal – it is also a conduit of counterhegemony. As his counterhegemonic educational agent, Gramsci names the "organic intellectual": an identity that expresses the "intellectual activity that exists in everyone at a certain state of development" (Gramsci 1971, 9). *Everyone* has the potential to learn about alternatives *and enact them* at the personal level. For change to happen, in any context, conditions must be developed which nurture an organic intellectual stratum, as part of the self-transformation which will mean that "every citizen can govern", or at least places him or her "in a general condition to achieve this [capacity]" (*ibid*, 40). Mobilising this power does not just involve communication, and "consist in eloquence, which is an exterior and momentary mover of feelings and passions" (*ibid*, 10), but requires *activity*, oriented towards the "building of an alternative culture, one through which the values and aspirations of a class can be expressed" (Adamson 1980, 42). This "alternative culture" would be supported by what Landry et al (1985) called a *radical infrastructure* – a way of organising information and non-informational resources in ways that make them useful for organic intellectuals.

Gramsci's model of hegemony and counterhegemony helps illuminate the kind of work Hamelink is advocating. What this involves in detail, intellectually, practically and educationally – and what role IL plays here – requires further discussion. Elaborating this argument simultaneously develops a radical IL. Radical IL contributes to the development of a counterhegemonic information infrastructure, through supporting and, where necessary, transforming context-specific ways of thinking and making decisions that more widely distribute authority over informational resources.

* * *

Hamelink's ideas are underdeveloped. His paper presented key concepts, but no more, and no work done with it since has enhanced his framework. Most subsequent citations are in literature reviews (e.g. Pinto et al 2013; Dudziak 2010 [in Portuguese]). Bawden's comprehensive review (2001) mentions Hamelink in passing as an example of media literacy. Downing (1988) and Kenny (2009) invoke his work in the same field. At the UNESCO/IFLA conference on Media and Information Literacy, Kurbanoğlu (2012) cited Hamelink, but still as an example of media literacy rather than IL, though the conference aimed to bring both areas together.

One could debate whether Hamelink should be assigned to the 'media literacy' school rather than 'information literacy', but I suggest the distinction is irrelevant. It should already be clear that a radical IL must attend to the hegemonic role of the broadcast media. Luyt and Azura (2010, no pagination) discuss how IL could become a tool of hegemony, and these include a lack of attention to:

> (T)he use of information literacy to push the norms of intellectual property protection... the effects produced by a lack of attention to media monopolization in information literacy initiatives... [and] by not challenging the positivist conception of knowledge that animates much of the library and information field, oppression is further enabled as it continues a tradition in educational institutions of ignoring the conditions of textual production, which allows the work of bureaucratic inscription to continue unimpeded.

'Media literacy' should not be discarded as a term, for the same reasons that scientific literacy, financial literacy, or visual literacy should not (Norton 2008). Instead, each 'multiliteracy' can be seen as a particular application of a wider discipline: information literacy.

O'Farrill (2008, 167) suggests dropping the term 'information' from IL altogether, asking:

> (C)an *The Seven Faces of Information Literacy* (Bruce 1997) be conceived of as The Seven Faces of Literacy?.... Can we think of workplace literacy rather than of workplace information literacy? If we answer 'yes' to these questions, we are agreeing that information literacy is just an aspect of literacy, or rather, that literacy means engaging with information in all of its modalities.

Here, the 'I' in IL will be retained, but O'Farrill's point is salient. The themes and practices of radical IL deal with communication as a whole, while at the same time foregrounding the importance of context. Thus, media literacy can be defined as information literacy with a specific focus on the texts, structures, and values of the broadcast media: *radical* media literacy would attend to the concentration of authority over this media, and the production of texts for distribution through alternative, more democratic channels. Scientific literacy can be defined as information literacy with a specific focus on the texts, structures, and values of the scientific establishment: *radical* scientific literacy would focus on how authority is or is not distributed through these media[3]. And so on (cf. Thompson 2007).

This is why IL explicitly transcends technology. Digital or ICT literacy should also be seen as subsets of information literacy. Information processing is fundamental to humanity. Information technologies – that is, means for recording and processing information (Bawden 2001, 96), which include cognitive tools such as methodologies and logic – long predate the computer (Grafstein 2007). Technology is *congealed cognitive authority* of one form or another, manifesting various conceptions of democracy, organisation, and information exchange (Williams and Edge 1996). "Social practices and technologies mutually constitute each other" (Tuominen et al 2005, 338). Technologies, in this perspective, count as text, as parts of the information landscapes within which we all must act. A radical IL should provide tools to help with the scrutiny of claims made by an information system, just as with any other text (cf. Shapiro and Hughes 1996).

As noted earlier, scrutiny of this kind is a learning process, and if the outcome of this learning is the creation of one's own knowledge, an information landscape that is relevant to oneself, this is empowering. Snavely and Cooper (1997, 11) suggest using the term "information empowerment" instead of IL, but admit that though "[i]nformation empowerment is an admirable goal... objections arise immediately when used in context. 'An information empowerment program'... brings groans from many who hear the phrase." Hepworth and Walton (2009, 3) clearly link IL with a more general empowerment of the literate population: better information leads to better choices, use of resources, and so on. Government rhetoric at least pays some lip service to this, with democratic theory founded on the notion of access to information in order to inform choices (as noted by Zurkowski). This kind of work does not need to be specifically termed 'IL' to be empowering. What Hamelink is talking about is a tendency, just as democracy and counterhegemony are tendencies that do not need to be named explicitly in a given discourse. One can, clearly, be acting in a fundamentally democratic way without having to explicitly invoke that term to describe what one is doing. The same is true of information literacy, which may arise in many situations yet not be explicitly invoked. Indeed, it is when the term IL is reserved only for a much more specific set of practices that its *institutionalisation* can be said to begin: a claim explored in more detail in chapters 3 and 4.

The three branches of the IL tree, epitomised by Zurkowski, Burchinal and Hamelink, have not grown into completely separate organisms. Their growth has intertwined them, and sometimes they can be seen as one. Like real trees, when looking at the whole, one sees a fractal entity, a mass of branches, twigs and leaves, but when one examines more closely, a pattern of growth can be discerned. External environmental factors have also played a part in how the tree has developed. Chapter 3 carries the narrative of this development forward into the 1980s and 1990s, the period of time over which the task of *defining* IL – of bringing the embryonic visions of Zurkowski, Burchinal, and Hamelink into more concrete form – largely took place.

Notes

1. He updated the review with two later papers (2007a; 2007b).
2. This author, even with the help of his university library, found it difficult to locate a copy for consultation. The British Library would not allow the

document outside their reference library, implying they hold the UK's only copy. To facilitate further scholarship, a digital version has been made available at *http://personalpages.manchester.ac.uk/staff/drew.whitworth/burchinal.html* with the permission of Texas A & M University and Prof Burchinal.

3. As already discussed in chapter 1, this is not advocating the dismantling of the structures of scientific method, nor the valourising of counterknowledge (Thompson 2008), but of understanding how science is dialogic and giving critical attention to how 'objectivity' is asserted within it.

3

The diversity of IL

Abstract: This chapter investigates how IL developed through the 1980s and 1990s, focusing on three particular strands of the narrative: the advocacy of the US library profession and the development of the first IL standards; the work of Carol Kuhlthau on information anxiety, psychology, and the role librarians can play as information mediators; and the work of those who have investigated IL through a phenomenographical lens, particularly Christine Bruce. The chapter concludes with a discussion of the importance of this latter field, which reveals the diversity of IL and the importance of experiencing variation within a context, as a learning tool.

Key Words: Standards, mediation, psychology, personal constructs, phenomenography, experience of variation, outcome space

Chapter 2 reviewed early moves towards defining information literacy, and argued that IL, from the start, was used to describe diverse ways of thinking and acting in the world. This chapter continues that story into the 1980s and 1990s, during which time IL moved from obscurity to become a common reference within LIS, standards were developed, and investigations took place into the role of the academic library in delivering IL. Particular attention is here paid to the work of two authors who have done much to draw attention to IL's *personal* dimensions: Carol Kuhlthau, whose work brings a psychological dimension into IL, but remains rooted in the specific context of library use, and Christine Bruce, whose work (along with associates such as Lupton, Edwards, and Partridge) has drawn on phenomenography as a methodology for studying and practising IL. Both view IL as a continuous activity, rather than a series of one-off information searches (cf. Taylor 1979, cited in Behrens 1994, 311), and Bruce, more than Kuhlthau, sees information literacy as something that is non-linear, multifaceted and rooted in general processes of learning, rather than the library specifically. IL, for Bruce, is a complex of ways of experiencing information that include objective and generic rules or standards but also personal and collective matrices of interpretation. These ideas are explored throughout this chapter.

The history of how the ACRL information literacy standards were developed in the US has been frequently told (once again Behrens (1994) provides an excellent review). For some, this *is* the history of IL: certainly it is treated as the dominant strand. Eisenberg, Lowe, and Spitzer's history (2004) begins with immediate citations of Zurkowski, Burchinal, then Owens; it then summarises developments from the 1989 ALA report on. There is no mention of Hamelink, nor any other developments between 1976 and 1989. The authors' perspective is clear from this passage (Eisenberg et al 2004, 11):

> Whatever our personal definition of information literacy may be, it is likely to stem from the definition offered in the *Final Report* of the American Library Association Presidential Committee on Information Literacy... (1989, p.1). As we have seen, this definition is reflective not only of the work of Zurkowski but of others who have sought to shape the concept.

The most significant trend of the 1980s and 1990s to which IL responded was that use of a computer (or terminal) to access information moved from specialist locations (libraries, universities, or information providers like those listed by Zurkowski), and came into the home. By 1999 the world anticipated by Burchinal (1976, 11), where banking, purchasing, and communications had become home- and computer-based, was a reality. These changes required the development of new skills in the general population, as noted by Demo (1986). Unlike Burchinal and Zurkowski, Demo could draw on detailed working definitions of IL, particularly those emanating from the Auraria library of the University of Colorado (Behrens 1994, 312). Their schema recognised that IL was more than just information retrieval, but also encompassed understanding and use, and that though IL complemented digital or computer literacy, it was not the same. For Behrens (*ibid*, 313), the Auraria work suggested "the wide parameters of possible information resources, and implies that information seeking is not confined to locating information in libraries."

Yet it was libraries that retained ownership of the term IL. This became significant as the 1980s matured. A US report entitled *A Nation at Risk* (Gardner 1983), which drew a pessimistic picture of US education and future economic prospects, was strongly criticised by the LIS profession for omitting to mention the actual or potential role of libraries (Breivik and Gee 2006, 35):

> (L)ibraries remained all but invisible in the literature on the information society that began emerging in the 1980s.... Of all the education reform reports of the 1980s, only the 1986 Carnegie Foundation Report, *College*, gave substantive consideration to the role of libraries in addressing the challenges facing higher education.

Breivik became a leading voice in the profession's efforts to reverse this neglect. This bore some fruit later in the decade. She and Gee claim (*ibid*) that 1987, and the publication of *Libraries and the Search for Academic Excellence*, was the "initial attempt by leaders in higher education and librarianship to look beneath surface impressions and consider a greater institutional role for libraries". IL was adopted as the standard bearer for this campaign. It was identified as the added value that the library could bring, not just to a university and its students but also the learning infrastructure of society as a whole. IL was seen by Breivik and her colleagues as a necessary skill "for integrated learning and preparation for lifelong learning and active citizenship" (*ibid, 40*) and these, in turn, are "the proper focus for quality undergraduate education in an information society" (*ibid*). Libraries offered the best environment for IL to be both developed and applied: "Libraries provide a model for the information environment in which graduates will need to work and live. Libraries offer a natural environment for problem-solving within the unlimited universe of information" (*ibid*). In this worldview, the road to information literacy lay through the library, epitomised by the title of Gwyer, Stubbings, and Walton's (2012) collection of papers from the 2012 IFLA Satellite conference on IL: *The Road to Information Literacy: Librarians as facilitators of learning*. Libraries offered the institution a broad "strategic edge", supporting not just teaching and learning, but administration, community service, and revenue-raising (Breivik and Gee 2006).

This evangelising resulted in the development of the ALA (1989), then ACRL (2000) standards for information literacy, which have driven IL practice and policy in the US ever since. The consequent focus in much literature is on developing assessment tools, or rubrics (e.g. Hoffmann and LaBonte 2012), the appropriate application of instructional design (e.g. Lavoie, Rosman and Sharma 2011), and new technological approaches (e.g. Kammer and Thompson 2011) to IL instruction, and integration with other curricula (e.g. Ragains 2001; Rockman 2004; many others).

In most of this literature, the ACRL standards drive practice, and the practice emerges within the academic library[1].

This view was criticised as early as 1991 by McCrank, who wondered whether IL was simply a "bandwagon" term that librarians were keen to claim without having considered the implications of adopting a pedagogical role. Badke has more than once (2008; 2012) bemoaned the isolation of IL in the library, considered a service subject if taught at all, not a credit-bearing discipline integrated with other curricula. There is plenty of work going on in the US that does not accord with this paradigm: for example, work by Chip Bruce in the largely Puerto Rican district of Paseo Boricua in Chicago (Bruce and Bishop 2008; chapter 8 below) and, at a more theoretical level, see Julien and Williamson (2011) amongst others. But while more needs to be said about the role IL plays within – and outside – the university, this is a discussion best left until the next chapter. For now, it is useful to review how IL developed elsewhere in the world during this period.

***

The IL literature from the United Kingdom draws on a more critical and exploratory tradition than the US, while nevertheless remaining centred in formal education. UK-specific IL standards exist, and are library-oriented, developed under the aegis of SCONUL, the Standing Conference of National and University Libraries (1999). While these tend to be interpreted and applied more loosely than the ACRL standards in the US, they remain linear. They assume that the highest-order thinking skills, and the development of critical knowledge, are only possible in the most advanced learners; that is, postgraduate students (see the critique of the ACRL, SCONUL and ANZIIL [Australia and New Zealand] standards in Andretta 2005, 41–54). The problem with this is (*ibid*, 48):

> This perspective... is not always confirmed by practice, as the level of competence of each learner is not dictated by his or her academic status but by the individual learner's ability to engage with complex problem-solving conditions and their capacity for independent learning at the outset.

What Andretta also neglects to mention is that these conditions may be met by – or developed in – learners outside the HE system. They will be outside it either because they cannot gain access to it, or because their query or area of interest is not something that formalised HE concerns itself with (for example, 'how to save a local woodland from being cleared for development').

This focus on HE, as in the US, characterises much of UK IL, bar a few exceptions (e.g. Crawford and Irving 2011). The area where the UK differs most from the US is in IL pedagogy. There is a strongly constructivist and, at times, critical pedagogical tradition in the UK (this being true of HE pedagogy more generally, at least in terms of the literature, if not always practice (Fry, Ketteridge and Marshall 1999)). Several IL teaching 'handbooks' have emerged, but these rely less on instructional design, rubrics, and published standards, and more on interpretive, holistic approaches such as inquiry-based learning (e.g. Hepworth and Walton 2009; Andretta 2005; 2012; Whitworth, Fishwick and McIndoe 2011). Innovation in pedagogy, as in the US, also extends to the use of technologies such as Second Life (Webber 2010) and, generally, there is a close relationship between IL and digital literacy (Markless 2009; Beetham, McGill and Littlejohn 2009). In the UK, however, practitioners feel the same sense of isolation from academic colleagues as elsewhere, and the UK government has never set national-level policies, or even made statements, on IL.

A recent publication edited by Secker and Coonan (2013) reflects many characteristics of the UK IL literature. This collection contains 10 chapters which collectively discuss how the subject matter of an IL course could expand beyond information retrieval, but while there is mention made, in the introduction, of the importance of the school sector, every chapter is based on an HE case. There is a sense of familiarity to the pleas in the introduction (Secker and Coonan 2013, xvi): "...if you are a librarian reading this book we urge you to pass it on to a teacher or a lecturer, or better still a principal or dean or even an education policy maker...", followed by this lament (*ibid*, xviii):

(I)n rethinking information literacy we must recognize that librarians are not islands in the education sphere. Neither are they the owners of 'information literacy'. That may be seen by some as revolutionary, but if we are truly committed to information literacy we will recognize that it is too important to remain the preserve of the library. We must seek out partnerships to work interprofessionally in our schools, colleges and universities. We must ensure that the new curriculum for information literacy has support at the highest level in our organizations. And we must lobby policy makers to ensure that governments recognize the central importance of information literacy in learning...

Like Badke's work (2008; 2012) this reads like an oration from a politician, a "call to arms" (Pope and Walton use this phrase directly: 2011, 8). Yet, it is little different from pleas made in the 1980s for a more holistic and integrated approach to teaching these skills, and for the bridging of gaps between librarians and academics. Pope and Walton (2011) take a pragmatic view, talking of "infiltrating the curriculum": integration with HE curricula is still the aim, but they are more prepared to acknowledge the impact of differences in perspective and how these affect the receipt of IL outside the teacher/librarian community (Pope and Walton 2011, 10):

> (I)nformation literacy is about deep learning, participation and making a real contribution leading to an enriched and empowered population... but therein lies an identity crisis aptly identified by Thornton (2010) who sees a real disconnect between how we (the librarian and information professional) see IL and how the rest of the world perceives it... 'a few dull lessons taken by a librarian as part of a – probably rather dull – research skills module, rather than a vehicle of empowerment and political liberation' (Thornton 2010, 8).

Pope and Walton advocate that librarians "become equal and involved", "stop wondering whether we are librarians or teachers" and ask what "they can uniquely bring to the business of educating employable graduates and fostering a real sense of economic and political engagement" (Pope and Walton 2011, 11). These are laudable aims, and the work of IL advocates mentioned throughout this section, and presented in conferences such as LILAC (the Librarians' Information Literacy Annual Conference: *www.lilacconference.com*) shows that the UK IL tradition is a healthy one. Yet despite its constructivist and innovative pedagogical tradition, and its clear desire to integrate, it has failed to break out of the library and HE sector in any significant way. Even within this sector IL's clear contribution to documents such as the Researcher Development Framework[2] is not directly cited, and the experience of its most active advocates has been represented more by frustration than progress (Andretta 2011). (A possible exception is Hepworth and Walton 2009).

Is IL *innately* a library domain? Does its having emerged from LIS result in it being so wedded to the assumptions of that discipline that bridges to others cannot be built? It may be tempting to conclude this, but none of the three seminal papers mentioned libraries directly. Only Burchinal mentioned HE, and there noted that any teaching role in IL should quickly be handed to schools. Yet the library/HE theme is beginning to seem dominant in the US and UK literature. In both locations, IL has become almost entirely the concern of libraries in HE, and even within these there is a sense of disconnection and a lack of outside integration.

To cover developments in the rest of the world in a brief section may assert a typical Anglo-American bias. A defence can be offered, however. Developments in two other countries, Sweden and Australia, will be discussed in detail after this point, with IL research from these two countries forming the basis of radical IL. Chapter 4 will conduct an analysis of literature from around the world, and the present author has already undertaken a review of IL (Whitworth 2010) which suggested that key themes from the UK and US contexts were just as present elsewhere, in locations as diverse as Finland, Hong Kong, and South Africa. Empirically, the ACRL standards, and the forms of thinking which underpin them, *do* have a strong influence on IL policies worldwide, particularly outside Europe, though there also exist examples of work that attempts to find more locally-specific standards and ways of working (see chapter 8 of this book). The SCONUL standards have also spread abroad, including to South Africa (Tiemensma 2012). Papers presented at the 2012 IFLA Satellite conference on IL (Gwyer, Stubbings and Walton 2012) reinforce these assessments.

Although unfortunately dated now, Virkus's review (2003) remains an excellent source for tracing developments in Europe, and there also exists a repository of IL practice drawn from a range of European countries (Basili 2011). Some broad themes can be discerned in these different national traditions. Macevičiūte (2006) reviewed the literature from Russia and Lithuania, noting that though writers from this region and the 'Western' literature tend not to cite each other, there are notable similarities in their concerns, although in Russia/Lithuania, the idea that the information user can be a *collective* is more fully developed. The Nordic countries (Denmark, Iceland, Norway, Finland, and Sweden) share a common interest in social democratic pedagogy, with IL given more prominence here, including in policy, than is common elsewhere in the world (Lonka 2012; Tolonen and Toivonen 2010), although the much-lauded 'Finnish model', with IL recognised at national level to a degree that exceeds other countries (noted in page 6 of the Alexandria Proclamation (2006)), does not necessarily equate to a policy that supports all aspects of IL (Whitworth 2010). Through the provision of fora such as the *Nordic Journal of Information Literacy* (*http://noril.uib.no*) and the

Creating Knowledge conferences, a healthy IL community is sustained in Scandinavia. In other countries around Europe, particular 'champions' are apparent in the literature – at least, that which has been translated into English at this time – e.g. Špiranec and Zorica (2010) in Croatia, Pinto and associates in Spain (2013). Outside Europe there are pockets of activity in certain locations, including southern Africa, with a number of papers emerging from South Africa (de Boer, Bothma and du Toit 2012; Fourie 2011) and Botswana (Oladokun and Aina 2011). Taiwan (Chen, Lin and Chang 2011, Chang and Liu 2011) and Brazil (Tavares, Hepworth and Costa 2011) have also seen activity. International agencies such as UNESCO have played a clear role, having catalysed declarations such as the Alexandria Proclamation (2006), the Prague Declaration (2003), and the Moscow Declaration on Media and Information Literacy (2012). Statements like these serve a dual purpose: they connect IL to worldwide concerns such as human rights, development, poverty, and environmental sustainability (here see also Sturges and Gastinger 2010; Tavares et al 2011; and chapter 8 below), and assert that education is a means to an end, not an end-in-itself. In addition, the declarations serve as resources that practitioners can use for inspiration and to which, in principle, national governments should respond via new policies.

Yet this is difficult to translate into practice, even in countries which are sympathetic to these goals. Once again, common themes emerge worldwide (Whitworth 2010, 317–8):

> Ponjuan (2010) makes the general point that any national IL policy is challenging to implement because very few countries have experience working with the library and information science field as well as educational communities like teachers: the links between these different groups are weak in most places. Consequently, IL is rarely recognized at the highest political level, being "subsumed within an 'information society' agenda focusing primarily on the promotion and development of ICT skills and infrastructure" (Russell and O'Brien 2009, p. 102: see also Whitworth 2009).

This brief review of developments in the last three decades cannot adequately cover even the most significant papers. As well as reviews already cited, like Virkus (2003), the works of Mutch (1997), Rader (2002), Lundh et al (2013), Markless and Streatfield (2007), Aharony (2010), Pinto, Cordón and Diáz (2010), and Weiner (2011) are useful reviews or bibliographies of work in the field. There also exists a substantial sub-genre of work in IL in the medical and public health disciplines, including reviews by Wyer and Silva (2009), Fourie (2009), Frisch, Camerini, Diviani and Schulz (2011), and Ngoh (2009). Yet the sense of a relative dearth of work outside the library/HE nexus is enhanced by the intimate nature of the literature reviews carried out by Williamson and Asla (2009), into IL amongst the very old (drawing only on two projects), and Partridge, Bruce, and Tilley (2008), who look at community IL through reviews of just three papers. Within the HE library, much work outside the US and UK continues to reflect the same concerns, namely training in skills and competencies, developing rubrics or criteria for assessment, and trying to secure collaborations between libraries and academics.

It may seem irrelevant – or, viewed positively, as a sign of the strength and applicability of standards – that the ACRL definition of IL has a clear influence over IL teaching in, say, Taiwan (Lin, Cheng, Liao and Yen 2012) or Iran (Babalhavaeji, Isfandyari-Moghaddam, Aqili and Shakooii 2009). Yet standards direct practice in education by setting a definition of 'what should be', and thus, influencing what is looked for in educational outcomes, and ultimately, what is taught. By their nature, educational standards (and, more loosely, 'best practices') have two essential characteristics: they strive to be generic, not context-dependent; they are monologic, not dialogic. Yet standards nevertheless emerge from particular contexts, at particular times, and are driven by the assumptions and needs of their creators, not of those who may adopt the standards elsewhere. This does not make them valueless, but it does mean that for their worth to be validated, standards and practices must be *applied* by educational practitioners (Carr and Kemmis 1986) – in other words, these providers need to engage in a dialogue with the standards, following the application with evaluation, action, research, and the development of communities in which practices can be shared (Wenger 1998). To some extent, papers like those cited here are undertaking this research. Yet the application of generic theories or best practices must also be essentially subjective and intersubjective, involving reflection and personal development, discussion, and the sharing of insights with colleagues (Carr and Kemmis 1986). Whitworth (2012) goes into more detail about the role of reflective practice in the professional development of the IL educator, and practical examples are offered by, for example, Fourie (2011), who uses mind maps. The process attends not just to the evaluation of practices that are oriented towards meeting specified goals, but also to paying critical attention to those goals, and review of them where necessary.

This is the distinction explored by Argyris and Schön (1999), who call the first approach *single-loop learning* and the latter *double-loop learning*. In double-loop learning, the relevance of the justifications and goals of an act are questioned, whereas in single-loop learning, only the actions are questioned, with justifications and goals left unscrutinised. In the IL literature, double-loop learning – meaning, here, investigation and research into the fundamental postulates of IL – does emerge, but this review has suggested that the majority of work is single-loop, assessing work being done to teach students in HE, through the library, to better accord with IL standards. This suggestion can be further supported through more quantitative methods of analysis, but that will be left until chapter 4.

***

IL was never conceived as a wholly technical project: Zurkowski, Burchinal and Hamelink, to varying degrees, differentiated IL from IS by introducing a *non-systematisable* human element. That is, seeing people not as akin to components in a machine or information system, but as manifesting essential aspects of knowledge formation which cannot be systematised. Intuition, psychology, affect, emotion, chance and, most of all, creativity are aspects of the human condition where control breaks down. They introduce unpredictability into decision-making, action and knowledge formation, and help explain not only the subjective, personal aspects of information processing, but intersubjective ones as well (Edwards 2006, 25).

The work of Carol Kuhlthau, particularly her book *Seeking Meaning* (1993), is the best example of a psychological approach to IL (and LIS more broadly). It was claimed by Julien and Williamson (2011) to be one of the few, perhaps the only, extant attempts to bring together the disciplines of information seeking (focused on by information scientists) and IL (focused on by practitioners), and to integrate psychology into IL, as called for by Marcum (2002) amongst others. In her introduction, Kuhlthau (1993, xvii-xviii) notes that librarianship is a practice-oriented field, and her work is an attempt to define theories on which the practice can become based. She critiques studies of the library which examine the effectiveness of the library *qua* system, judged through quantitative evaluations (financial health, footfall, large-scale surveys, percentage of searches which were successful, etc) (*ibid*, 79). Instead she calls for, and conducts, user-focused studies, to give deeper insight into the personal motivations and qualities affecting user interactions (*ibid*, 80). Through these studies, she transcends the emphasis on *cognitive* change that characterises work in IL pedagogy, to consider learning and information use as also involving *affective* change. Recognising this, her aim is to explore how library practices can accommodate the psychology of information seeking.

Kuhlthau's foundation is the Personal Construct Psychology (PCP) of George Kelly (1963). Kelly added an affective dimension to theories of thinking and learning by finding ways to observe this dimension (Kuhlthau 1993, xix). Adding this dimension means that for Kelly, and thus Kuhlthau, cognitive change, affective change, and changes in actions are a unified whole (Kuhlthau 1993, p. 26). Thus, so are *learning* and *transformation* at the personal scale (*ibid*, xix):

> Our view of the world is constantly being constructed by new experiences. This process begins with uncertainty which increases as we encounter inconsistencies and incompatibilities within the new information itself and with our previously established constructs. Construction takes place through a process of formulating tentative hypotheses for testing, assessing, defining, refining, and reconstruing. Ultimately, new constructs are formed; these alter and expand the existing system – in other words, we learn.

The personal constructs that shape our experience of learning and transformation can therefore be considered forms of cognitive authority: they are "integrated, organized representation[s] of past behaviour and experience which guide individuals in reconstructing previously encountered material..." (*ibid*, 24 via Bruner 1973, 5). Constructs shape how new experiences are received, and if there is conflict between existing constructs (authorities) and new experiences (information), uncertainty will be enhanced. Consequences may include anxiety, or other negative psychological effects including denial, anger, and confusion (Fransella and Dalton 2000, 39–43).

But though these constructs are sometimes explicit, more often they are unarticulated, and thus concealed. Any personal construct is a *way of thinking*: a methodology from which springs methods and structures for processing information (Kuhlthau 1993, 185): "Recall is based on our former constructs (world view) which form a frame of reference for selective remembering." But (*ibid*, 20): the "constructs that we have formed are not easily discarded...". These can hamper the receipt of challenging new information. We may avoid the change or challenge, entrenching around existing constructs and reaffirming them, becoming "stuck" (Fransella and Dalton 2000, 14) with a way of thinking that is not necessarily appropriate for changed circumstances.

An example of a construct would be 'I am healthy'. This will probably have originated – perhaps some time before – as a valid and rational assessment of an individual's physical condition. But if it becomes a construct, that person may reject information – pain, a lump – that might challenge it (a cognitive bias: see Blaug 2007, 30–1; Evans 1989). Concern from a family member, however well-meaning, may be ignored for the same reason. Even a medical diagnosis may not alter behaviour. Counselling may help, or self-reflection, but it may be that the construct never changes.

Kelly's is an applied theory. A psychologist using PCP plays an active role, helping the subject establish how personal constructs can block change. Learning about the constructs and learning about the change come at the same time, and it is the role of the PC psychologist to help with the transformation, raising awareness in the individual about their cognitive structures. The psychologist can use a variety of techniques to reveal these constructs to the subject. The repertory grid is one validated approach (Fransella and Dalton 2000, 51*ff*) but Fransella, who has done a great deal to develop Kelly's work, is insistent that no specific technique is prescribed. (Chapter 8 presents examples.)

Kuhlthau uses PCP to reveal stages in the information seeking process, and the impact of affect or emotion at each stage. Her hypothesis is that (1993, xx): "information seeking is a process of construction that begins with uncertainty and anxiety." From the early stages of the process, where the user anticipates the task, preparing for the work ahead both cognitively (by contemplating possible topics for the search, brainstorming ideas) and affectively (feeling apprehensive, uncertain), through to what Kuhlthau calls the "pre-focus exploration" stage, the user's cognitive work will likely be accompanied by feelings of confusion and doubt. Apprehension may prevent the search from commencing altogether. Once these stages are passed, however, and a *focus* for the information search has been formulated (whether through a "sudden moment of insight" (*ibid*, 48) or more gradually, through exploration of the literature in the broader area), Kuhlthau suggests that a more optimistic and confident mindset is generated in the user, and increased interest (*ibid*, 46–52). Focus formulation is therefore seen by Kuhlthau as the most significant stage or task, and depends on exploration, and a tolerance for uncertainty (*ibid*, 114–5). Kuhlthau also notes, however, that (*ibid*, 115):

(U)sers often move directly from selecting a general topic or area to the task of collecting information, skipping over the important stage of exploration altogether. Exploratory acts uncover information for formulating new constructs, whereas collecting acts gather information for documenting established constructs.

This last sentence directly reflects the difference between double- and single-loop learning, and also explains why exploration and focus formulation are also those areas which promote the most anxiety, as they are where the new constructs are formed. Therefore, an IL pedagogy that focuses on mere retrieval of information is not promoting creativity, *because* it is systematised: because it avoids dealing with uncertainty (*ibid*, 172). Uncertainty, and hence anxiety, cannot be relieved by the design of a better information system, nor better teaching – just as the construct 'I am healthy' may not even be challenged by a professional diagnosis. Uncertainty is more likely a *response* to design or to certain types of teaching (IL, or otherwise).

Thus, information literacy must allow for personal constructs, which contribute to the possible rejection of information, even specifically relevant information. Some constructivist and critical IL pedagogies do address these matters (see, for example, Shor 1996). However, Kuhlthau is not claiming to offer new insights into pedagogy. Rather, she seeks to integrate psychological issues and the subjective domain into LIS. Through doing so, she shows how 'information anxiety' is not a failure of the user, a pathology caused by poor education or apathy; it is instead a natural part of the human condition.

Her response is to address, not teaching, but *mediation*. Mediators play an important role in the information search process. These may be information professionals, such as librarians or teachers, or they may be friends, or texts such as books, newspaper articles or TV programmes. All may help a learner focus their attention on specific elements of their information search by suggesting ways to proceed, and thus, achieve better focus. Mediation helps the learner through the 'zone of intervention' – "that area in which a user can do with guidance and assistance what he or she could not do alone" (*ibid*, 176; via Vygotsky 1978). The assistance has to be dynamic, constantly reviewing and revising itself, because the zone of intervention alters as the nature of the user's search, and their knowledge and practices, change. Intervention in areas that lie outside the 'zone' may be "intrusive on the one side [if the student has already changed practice], overwhelming on the other" (p. 176). Thus, the mediator and student are ideally in a constant *dialogue*, each adapting their position with reference to the other (Linell 2009, 86; Laurillard 2002). This complex dance of diagnosis and intervention requires constant reflection-in-action "in which the practitioner relies not only on the patterns and underlying principles of a theoretical framework but also on sound professional experience" (*ibid*, 177).

Effective mediation has to handle uncertainty, however, and "[u]ncertainty, the predominant experience in the early stages of the search process, is not being sufficiently addressed in library and information services" (1993, p. 172). Mediation, for Kuhlthau, is still largely seen in LIS as a technical issue (design of systems), or a cognitive one (design of pedagogy), not an affective one. Affect requires the mediator to take on a counselling role: specifically, to help the user reveal personal constructs that are impacting on the search.

Kuhlthau recognises various levels of mediation, but only the highest level involves true counselling. In the first three levels (*ibid*, 137–142) – seeing the library as an *organiser* of information at level 1, a *locator* at level 2, and *identifier* at level 3 – only one point of contact between user and library system is expected. In consequence, the encounter can become automated. The user makes a request, the system delivers a single result (a single resource at the organizer and locator levels, a single list of resources at the identifier level), and the conversation is over. At Kuhlthau's level 4 – *advisor* – a more complex result is returned, but the implication still remains, that the enquiry is complete. A *sequence of information-searching activity* is outlined, but there is still a singularity to it. Thus, again, there is the potential to automate this type of mediation.

However, at level 5 of mediation, the *counsellor*, the user's experience is considered more holistically, their learning allowed for. There is no expectation that a single response will be made to the user's request, nor that no further contribution from the user will be required. Rather than returning a result, the counsellor "establishes a dialogue" (144), a way "to enable people to explore new ideas" (154): the dialogue is open-ended, and not finalised after the delivery of the resource. What is being offered at level 5 is not information, or even meaning, but *guidance for the user, in their own personal process of seeking meaning* (*ibid*, 143):

> The recommended sequence of sources of information emerges as the topic or problem evolves in a highly individual way. The information is understood from the frame of reference of the user's past experience and the constructs they hold.... The Counsellor approaches information seeking as a creative, individual process that is dynamic and unique for each person.

The role does not have to be instantiated in only a single person or office. An effective *infrastructure* for counselling may be developed, integrating the work of many different professionals: teachers, administrators, librarians, and educators (*ibid*, 151). This is a view of IL as being, not a response to the design of an information system, but *instantiated within it* – the system being designed not only to deliver information but promote its own effective use. It is a worthy view.

The problems with Kuhlthau's work, however, vis-à-vis the development of radical IL, are that these insights remain rooted within the library context, most obviously within higher education. This is evident from her methodology. The library users from whom Kuhlthau gathered data were students, usually seeking information to complete an assignment. This is only one kind of 'information need', and can be considered as an "abstraction forced on the student" (Edwards 2006, 36: cf Saracevic 2007b). Would the same feelings of anxiety be present in library users engaged in entirely different search tasks?

More broadly, despite advocating changes in practice, and discussing, albeit briefly, how this transformation could be attended to (via reflective practice: Kuhlthau 1993, 177), the paradigm of IL as being an outgrowth of bibliographic instruction, and thus, located within the library, is not questioned. Kuhlthau sees *cognitive authority* as still invested in the system, or library-as-text, and the expertise of the individual, professional librarian. Arguably, she sees anxiety and uncertainty as things which block, not learning as such, but *use of the library*. It is clearly stated that the theory she is developing is a "process theory for library and information services" (*ibid*, xxiii); the aim is to understand uncertainty and anxiety, but as additional inputs into the system. She says (*ibid*, xxv) that "this book is written as a tool for reflective librarians and information professionals to articulate a theoretical perspective for designing intervention services that recognize and respond to users' needs for counselling in the process of learning from information access and use." Uncertainty, at least in principle, can be accommodated in a system (*ibid*, 108, via Bates 1986; see also "soft systems methodology" (Checkland and Holwell 1998)), and she notes (*ibid*, 133) that "after a problem has been well-defined and formulated, the library system works fairly efficiently". What she is trying to do is seek a fuller problem definition, a way for the library system to accommodate the uncertainty of the earlier stages, and help the user reach a point, after which they would be able to use the library system without further difficulty.

There is also the implication that the information sources will *in principle* be held in a library. With this single sentence (*ibid*, 153, emphasis added), Kuhlthau states what her limits are: "The broader view of information education enables students to learn how to learn *in the library*." This means that structural elements in the landscape are not considered – *including the library itself*. What this perspective does not account for are cognitive conflicts between the library and its users. Students do not necessarily have the cognitive architecture to engage with the library in this way. The students that she researched "lacked constructs that would prompt them to request mediation from a librarian" (*ibid*, 129), even for simple tasks such as information collection. The library was seen as a self-service environment, and seeking help from a librarian was not judged a wholly "legitimate" approach to researching a topic (*ibid*, 130). Elmborg (2002) observed how students are unfamiliar with the conventions of the reference interview. Thus it may be their encounter with the library itself that foments anxiety, rather than their understanding of the material found.

In the end, though her work is a valuable statement of the links between learning and transformation at a *subjective* level, Kuhlthau never really moves beyond the subjective. Her theoretical focus remains on the individual user and their psychology, and the need to see this psychology as a form of data, an input into the system; something which, if only it were understood better, would contribute to the transformation of library practice. She does not account for the impact of the institutionalisation of IL, *the way that changes in user education may come to challenge the constructs on which librarianship is based* - and which may therefore be deflected, denied, and absorbed by similar processes as Kelly describes, but this time acting at the intersubjective level.

Essentially, the library – or any other IL educator – needs to account for its own cognitive structures. Personal constructs can be intersubjectively maintained, a response to ways of thinking that may have been embedded in technology, creating the sort of cognitive conflicts that provoke learning in the first place. To understand any such constructs it is necessary to engage in double-loop learning. PCP is explicit about how this works at the individual level (Fransella and Dalton 2000), but the transformation of any working practice also requires this level of reflection among a collective, as well.

Nevertheless, Kuhlthau's work is important. She makes key connections between learning and transformation, standing on a wider theoretical base than LIS had previously. PCP helps IL educators understand not just how anxiety and uncertainty can be designed for, but how identities are formed, information needs provoked or repressed, and ideologies and assumptions which drive action can be hidden, even to the person holding them and undertaking the activity (Russell 2003, 126).

* * *

With such a multiplicity of personal constructs, perceptions, and actions influencing communication, it should be clear that IL cannot be generic. What information is important and relevant, what forms of authority pertain in a given place and time – these will all differ from landscape to landscape, and thus it is reasonable to state that IL will also differ. At the same time, one cannot ignore normative issues. In the end, IL is about *making judgements* of one sort or another, and if these judgements are themselves to be judged then some kind of normative core must remain, without this being simply a way of seeing one form of IL or other practice as 'correct' or 'standard' and privileging it over others.

What IL therefore needs are *normative foundations for plurality.* Securing these normative foundations must begin by establishing the plurality of views of information and IL. This has been done well by researchers working within the phenomenographic tradition. Phenomenography is named as one of the three key theories of IL by Limberg et al (2012), along with sociocultural practice theory (discussed in this book in chapter 7), and Foucauldian discourse analysis (not discussed directly, but the work on Bakhtin in chapter 6 takes up a similar task). An excellent review of phenomenography's contribution to IL research is also contributed by Andretta (2007b).

Phenomenography[3] is a research methodology that emerged from work done in Sweden by Marton (1981). It was originally applied to the study of IL by Bruce (1997) and subsequently extended by her and other colleagues at the Queensland University of Technology (e.g. Bruce 2008; Lupton 2004; Hughes, Bruce and Edwards 2007; Yates, Partridge and Bruce 2009; Gunton 2011; Sayyad Abdi, Partridge and Bruce 2013) and elsewhere (Smith and Hepworth 2012). In essence, it is a way of learning about variation in people's experience of some aspect of the world (Marton 1981); a methodology for understanding different ways of being aware of, or experiencing, a phenomenon and, through doing so, building a picture of a phenomenon as a whole. Phenomenography seeks not to make statements about the world (a 'first-order perspective'), but rather, statements about how other people experience their world (Edwards 2006, p. 53 via Marton 1981): the 'second-order perspective'. Its area of exploration is not how the individual makes meaning and learns, but how these things take place collectively, building on, but *transcending*, individual perceptions. Experience, and thus meaning, are formed within the relations that exist between people and their experienced world.

Bruce's key insight was to take this *research methodology* and, through applying it to IL, establish how revealing variation in information to learners can also be an *IL pedagogy*. Edwards provides the best summary of how this can be done (2006, 49):

> At the core of variation theory, and its influence on learning then, we must understand all the aspects or elements that are possible to be discerned in an experience, and understand the varying ways of experiencing the object of learning. Having done this we can then restructure the learning environment to encourage students to experience all the possible variations. If we wish to do this in our learning environments then phenomenography is the approach needed. We need to use phenomenography to understand and draw out the variation in the categories, and then we use variation theory to apply the identified variations in practice in our learning environment. Phenomenographic categories reveal the space of the variation, or, the varying ways of seeing the phenomenon. They also reveal the central focus of each experience and the different dimensions within the experience that are simultaneously noticed, or ignored. Having found the variations, and having identified the varying aspects in the group awareness, we can use them to identify ways to encourage people to discern another aspect of the experience, an aspect they have previously not discerned.

Though this is clearly a methodology, there is no emphasis placed on particular methods of gathering data. One can undertake phenomenographical research through surveys, hermeneutics (the analysis of text), in-depth research interviews, concept mapping, and so on. But whatever tool is used, the data gathering process must elicit variation, without imposing views of the phenomenon on informants. Whatever data is generated (*ibid*, 61):

> (T)he researcher develops the *categories of description* of the phenomenon. In other words, these categories are the researcher's interpretation, based on data analysis, of the variation in the group's account of the way they experience

the phenomenon.... Each category represents a sub-group, or conception, of the whole phenomenon; they represent one way in which the phenomenon is experienced.

Each category reflects a particular *structure of awareness* (Booth 1992); the meaning of the phenomenon, but one derived through concrete experience, things that have actually happened in the world rather than theoretical constructs. What is in particular *focus* in participants' structure of awareness? What is at the margins? What are the key categories? These are all 'moving streams'; core areas or themes are focused on, from within a more general 'thematic field' that has some marginal aspects. This notion was later refined into ideas of internal and external horizons (Marton, Dall'Alba and Beaty 1993).

These different categories of experiencing a phenomenon within a community of participants are manifested in the *outcome space* (Edwards 2006, p. 62):

> Having identified the categories of description and the corresponding structure of awareness, the next step in a phenomenographic study is the development of an *outcome space* to show the world, simply, your findings. That is, having identified the categories, a picture of the relationship between the categories found is drawn. In its simplest form, the outcome space is a map showing what critically different categories have been found by the research.

This picture may be graphic in form, but also textual, such as a table. Outcome spaces are not intended to amalgamate second-order perspectives into a first-order perspective: that is, to be a *definition* of a phenomenon. Rather, they are tools for exploring and revealing variation (Andretta 2007b, 156). Marton conceives of the outcome space as a *text* – a tabular or diagrammatic representation of some kind, which may be paper-based or digital (Edwards (2006) provides the best example of the latter; also Steinerová 2010). The space maps the variation in awareness of whatever aspect of the world is involved in the inquiry. Thus, an outcome space becomes a map of the collective experience of the phenomenon: *one possible map of the information landscape*. As differences are evident between maps of rural or mountainous landscapes (more commonly used by walkers, and therefore mapping features like contours, streams, fields) and maps of cities (aimed at drivers and so omitting those details, but emphasising roads), an outcome space will only focus on certain things. Or, emphasis may vary between elements of the outcome space, depending upon the audience for the space (map).

Russell (2003, 127) writes that phenomenography "is particularly useful for research in previously understudied areas... where one needs to do introductory work to ascertain the range of experiences." It is a "mapping method, which will point to areas, which need further, more detailed, exploration" (see also Wandersee 1990). In sum, it is a method of *raising awareness about variation within a context*.

The significant question for IL is what happens to the outcome space after this text has been produced. Bruce's move was toward using this awareness of variation as a teaching tool. This was a two-stage process. Firstly, her own outcome space was presented in several publications, such as Bruce (1997), which described what she called the "seven faces" of IL, these being categories describing different ways information is experienced: as information technology, information sources, information process, information control, knowledge construction, knowledge extension, and wisdom. It was then suggested that (*ibid*, 44):

> The seven faces of information literacy, and their corresponding workplace processes, provide a curriculum framework for information managers with an interest in training and educating their clientele to effectively use the organisation's information services, and for providers of beginning and continuing professional education. Understanding more about how information is effectively utilised by practising professionals is likely to help educators design a curriculum which is relevant and transferable to professional practice.

Similar claims can be made in other aspects of education, as well as workplace training. This interest in application drove Bruce to a more specific investigation of information literacy *education*. An investigation of how IL was taught needed to pull together other phenomenographical investigations, including participants' views of teaching and learning, as well as information and IL itself. This more multifaceted investigation was presented in Bruce et al (2006), the "six frames of information literacy education". Briefly, these frames are:

- *Content*: IL is knowledge about the world of information
- *Competency*: IL is a set of competencies or skills
- *Learning to learn*: IL is a way of learning

- *Personal relevance*: IL is learned in context and is different for different people/groups
- *Social impact*: IL issues are important to society
- *Relational*: IL is a complex of different ways of interacting with information.

A holistic programme of IL education would need to incorporate all of these to be effective (Whitworth et al 2011).

The relational frame is the most significant vis-à-vis IL pedagogy. Bruce et al suggest that the relational frame brings together, at least, the content and learning to learn frames (*ibid*, 42)[4]: "learning in this frame is understood as coming to discern things in new or more complex ways", and learning occurs when variation in ways of understanding or experiencing are revealed. This will "expand focal awareness" (Andretta 2007b, 156). Put more simply, it will give learners something new to think about. Personal constructs may, as noted above, lead to them rejecting the new information, but personal constructs can themselves be the focus of teaching in the relational frame.

The second part of Bruce et al (2006, 43–55) describes some case studies of relational IL teaching, and other authors have contributed similar investigations (e.g. Whitworth 2009b). Bruce also developed the model in her book (2008), *Informed Learning*, which "draws on contemporary HE teaching and learning theory to suggest ways forward to build a learning agenda that values the need for engaging with the wider world of information", offering practical teaching techniques that can be applied in academic disciplines, professions, communities, the workplace and the research community itself. The six frames have also been drawn on to analyse national IL policies (Whitworth 2010) and are used in chapter 4 below to assist the analysis of a selection of IL papers.

Other authors have used phenomenographic methods in different ways. Edwards (2006) sought to capture variation in how students searched for Internet information, with her four categories being "looking for a needle in a haystack", "finding a way through a maze", "using the tools as a filter", and "panning for gold". Edwards wants to look for triggers to help students move to a higher level of searching sophistication. Her digital outcome space, a Flash movie, is an exemplar of the idea (*http://www.netlenses.scitech.qut.edu.au/*). Yates has looked at health literacy through phenomenographic methods (e.g. Yates et al 2009), and O'Farrill (2008b) used it in a study of NHS-24, a telephone helpline, in Scotland.

* * *

Shenton and Hay-Gibson (2011, 167) call IL "among the ultimate in transdisciplinary phenomena", with transdisciplinarity being "essentially acontextual" and applicable across all different subjects, and Tomic (2010) sees in Bruce's work the potential for it to be considered an underlying philosophy of information, one that can unify studies of information behaviour, information retrieval, and critical thinking. So the stakes are high, and care is required before these claims can be endorsed.

The outcomes of phenomenographic enquiry should not be seen as *definitions* of any given field. Rather, they are categories of description drawn from one particular exploration. To treat them as indicating an end-point of some kind would be to reify them, turning them from contributions to a dialogue into monologic pronouncements. Instead, they should be seen as representations that suggest avenues of further exploration. This is what a good map does. Russell (2003, 128) argues that phenomenographic results permit "fellow researchers to analyze, then connect and contrast results with their own research, as well as make their own decisions about potential applications". As with any other text, these results can be tested by being opened to scrutiny and related to other investigations, other experiences of the phenomenon, to *collectively* judge whether there are mutual insights to be gained from the inquiry. Thus, the insights are validated, and may continue to evolve.

It is here that one can see the value of phenomenography to the dialogic view of IL being developed in this book. Inquiries that develop the experience of variation allow for the scrutiny of existing forms of cognitive authority in a particular landscape, by helping community members discern alternatives (Wilson 1983, 124): "Awareness of the existence of alternatives is the first step towards weakening the hold of cognitive monopolies." This does not mean that, nihilistically, every assertion of cognitive authority should be challenged. But it does mean that the teacher, the information professional, seeking ways to make their teaching more effective, can find methods for exploring and scrutinising the cognitive authorities which reside in a particular setting. To this end (Limberg et al 2012, 103): "phenomenographic categories of description are applicable as objects of learning to consciously use in collective interaction in classrooms and libraries in order to enable different views of information practices to diverge and be challenged."

Methodologically, then, the outcome space becomes an informational resource for further investigations of the phenomenon. Outcome spaces do not have to be 'texts' or 'diagrams' in a literal sense, and they certainly are unlikely to remain as such: they may become options on a computer menu or tick boxes on a rubric: in other words, reified aspects of an information system. Or, they may be kept at the forefront of awareness, used as resources for open reflection and discussion, and contribute to the transformation of a particular context. Thus, a link is made between learning and practice, within the phenomenographical paradigm.

This link is needed, because Säljö (1997) has argued against Marton's notion that experience is fundamental – that, as he put it in the title of a paper (Marton 1995) which answered an earlier critique of Säljö's (1994): "I experience, therefore I am". For Säljö, one's experience of something cannot in fact be separated from cultural practices. The phenomenographic research interview itself imposes an authority, of a sort, on the experience of variation that the interviewee is able to express. And even though this kind of formal research is not the only arena from which outcome spaces will emerge, not all experiences of variation will be welcomed, or treated equally. Some experiences of variation, certain categories, particular structures of awareness; these may be incompatible with existing cognitive authorities and the information systems in which they are embedded and, as a result, may be actively challenging to authority structures within an information landscape. These authorities may reassert themselves at various stages in the process of the enquiry: certain categories of description may be prevented from being expressed; outcomes may be ignored or repressed; the enquiry may be prevented from starting in the first place, either directly or indirectly (e.g., there is no workload allowance for professional development, no space in a standards-oriented IL curriculum). Users may be forced to fit the requirements of a system, and while this is not necessarily a disempowering process (depending on how the system has been designed), it will risk effacing context and thus the experience of variation. A more technical, and less user-centred, programme of education will, at best, be the result: at worst either the system may be rejected by the user or the value of their own context and understanding will be erased altogether.

Yet it must also be remembered that for knowledge to progress, as noted in chapter 1, there must always be *some* monologism, some way of fixing and asserting cognitive authority. The question is whether, within a given information landscape, such authority can be scrutinised *when necessary*.

Bearing these observations in mind, it is surprising that the notion of *critical phenomenography* has not gained more currency in the literature. The only reference found was by Russell (2003, 128), and that in passing. The reflective process that she describes helps the researcher become aware of the *ideologies* that lie within a context; a social system, a particular tool, or any other phenomenon open to phenomenographical enquiry. Thus, critical phenomenography addresses such questions as: What power structures are revealed within the phenomenon? How can the experience of variation be used to shed light on what is valued and what is not valued, and how does this understanding affect the usefulness of the outcome space as a subsequent resource for learning? These questions are aimed at preventing the products of phenomenographic investigation (outcome spaces) becoming concealed or repressed. John Dewey wrote that (1909, 48): "Most persons are unaware of the distinguishing peculiarities of their own mental habit. They take their own mental operations for granted and unconsciously make them the standard for judging the mental processes of others." A critical phenomenography would not only seek to reveal these hidden "mental operations" to learners, but also to investigate how such operations – through technologies, standards, procedures, and other cognitive authorities – are imposed from without, how they affect information exchange, and how authority structures built around them may be transformed.

O'Farrill attempts to make a connection between phenomenography and practice-based views of information landscapes, linking them via the notion of *critical realism*. The phenomenographic view risks being just interpretive, but this can be overcome if one sees social structures as real, not just perceived, influences over practice (O'Farrill 2008, 162). These structural elements are dynamic, but always "pre-date practices at a given point in time" (*ibid*). How, then, do these elements come to be, and why are some more likely to influence practice than others: in other words, why do they have more authority within information landscapes than others? Asking questions like these turns the inquiry into a critical one (cf. Fay 1975).

Phenomenography is only one possible approach to the study of IL, but it has proven a productive one. Engaging with it, particularly with a critical slant, focuses attention on the relationship between learning and transformation. Therefore, in the form of a critical phenomenography, it is a crucial pillar of radical IL.

* * *

Chapter 2 concluded that information is context-specific, and information literacy must account for this. What chapter 3 has done is suggest *how much* information is context-specific, right down to the micro- and individual levels. In turn, an individual may occupy multiple contexts. Learning takes place through – and therefore depends on – interacting with different contexts, and situations in which there is an element of uncertainty, but because of the ways we handle uncertainty, there is always a risk that instead of becoming a resource for learning, new information will be rejected. IL is about not only helping an individual retrieve information, therefore, but also helping them to understand it, absorb it, and learn from it.

Chapter 3 has also suggested that IL *itself* must be sensitive to the plurality of different contexts, without collapsing into relativism. Not all contexts are equal, and experiencing variation may be challenging to authority. Constructs, values, and assumptions which form significant parts of the exchange structures within one landscape may be antithetical to information exchanges in a different context, but if the relationship between these two contexts is unequal or hierarchical, they may come to shape activity in the second context in any case. This will stimulate learning, but if that learning results in challenges to the authorities rooted within the initial context, either the results of learning may be rejected, or the whole learning process suppressed. Chapter 4 will now go on to show how this kind of thing is not just something that happens outside IL, but also within it.

Notes

1. An informal quantification to be more fully justified in chapter 4.
2. See *http://www.vitae.ac.uk/researchers/428241/Researcher-Development-Framework.html*: a framework for developing the post-award employability of PhD students and researchers.
3. Not to be confused with phenomenology: a distinction summarised by Andretta (2007b, 153–4).
4. Whitworth et al (2011, 48) subsequently argued that the relational frame in fact brought together all five of the other frames.

4

The institutionalising of IL

Abstract: This chapter first undertakes a content analysis of a sample of IL literature published since 1990, in order to suggest that despite the range of potential approaches summarised in the last chapter, the field remains dominated by a perspective focused on higher education and competency-based approaches. This supports a conclusion that IL has become institutionalised within library and information science, and the academic library. This institutionalisation has damaged the development of IL, by neglecting community-based, intersubjective judgments about information, and maintaining a theory-practice gap.

Key Words: Institutionalisation, academic libraries, standards, monologism, theory-practice gap.

So far, this book has presented IL as based around sensitivity to different contexts and attending not only to the retrieval of information but its use, formulation, and (re-) production. An information literate person is not only competent at retrieving information, but is also able to understand possible variations between the context in which the information was produced and the context in which it must subsequently be understood and used. He/she would account for these differences when making judgements about the cognitive authority, relevance, and validity of the information. IL is aided by a facility with various tools for processing information, including ICT, but also encompassing other technologies, practices, ways of thinking, and defining words. The question of which of these tools are significant has answers that vary from context to context; therefore, these tools can, and should, themselves be read and judged as texts. Information literacy, therefore, becomes not just attention to particular texts at particular times, but also an ongoing process of nurturing the information landscapes within which individuals and their communities exist and learn. These things are direct consequences of the dialogic perspective.

Yet a great deal of IL literature and practice does not accord with this view. This statement will be justified by the opening section of this chapter, which conducts a relatively comprehensive, quantitative analysis of the IL literature that emerged after the publication of the first IL standards by the ALA (1989). Around what themes does the literature cluster? Conversely, what aspects of IL are neglected, why does this neglect matter, and how can it be explained? Answers to the latter question are sought in the phenomenon of *institutionalisation* (Douglas 1986). The chapter will conclude by suggesting that institutionalisation of a certain view of IL has damaged the whole field by neglecting *community-based* IL and also by creating, and maintaining, a *theory-practice gap* (Carr and Kemmis 1986). The existence of this gap in IL (Pilerot and Lindberg 2011) is evidence of the reasons why a radical IL is required, and helps illustrate the form it needs to take.

* * *

How does one conceptualise a phenomenon through an analysis of the research that has been done into that phenomenon? If the search is for intellectual themes, found via an in-depth, qualitative analysis, then the literature review is appropriate, conducted of either a few papers (as with chapter 2 above) or a larger number (as with chapter 3). But literature reviews, like other qualitative analyses, have to be selective (see Lundh et al 2013, for example). At the other extreme one can conduct analyses on large datasets using automated techniques like data mining. An example is Weiner's (2011) review of IL, encompassing around 16,000 papers. Other, systematic analyses of IL exist, using smaller but still comprehensive samples, e.g. Pinto et al (2010; 2013), Aharony (2010), Rader (2002); and see also Urquhart (2010), a meta-review, or 'review of reviews'. Each of these, as well as Stevens (2007), support the observation that IL research is skewed towards particular views of the subject and particular locations for its practice. Rader estimates, for example, that about 60% of all published IL research up to 2002 focused on HE. Aharony (2010) and Pinto et al (2010) both note that LIS remains the most common disciplinary classification for IL literature, though noted reasonably high proportions also in the health sector and the academic discipline of Education.

The review conducted here is not a systematic or a bibliometric review; that would add little to the work of these other authors. Nor is it a phenomenographic study, as no new outcome space is being sought, although it does pay homage to the tradition of hermeneutic phenomenography (Franz 1994), analysing texts that were created for other purposes and existed prior to the activity of the researcher. Hermeneutics, generally, is a research approach which seeks to understand a text and its interpretation as a single whole, building bridges between the intentions and perceptions of both author and reader, thus investigating variation in how texts are interpreted (Hasselgren and Beach 1997, 198). In hermeneutics, knowledge is dependent upon context and perspective. Texts are shaped by external factors. That is, any variation in them is not entirely innate, but also a factor of the shape of the general field; the *information landscape*. A critical perspective can be added by noting, as at the end of chapter 3, that variation in a landscape is not uniform, but 'lumpy'. Certain signs, definitions, and authorities will play more or less significant roles within it, directing practice, becoming embedded into technologies, and thus shaping meaning. The collective effect of such shaping could be considered hegemonic. Texts encode ideologies, and as revealing these is the aim of a critical study (Russell 2003), critical and hermeneutic approaches can complement one another.

A hermeneutic study, of a wider sample of texts than could be incorporated within a literature review, can produce quantitative data that might support qualitative assessments already made of the landscape under investigation: here, the academic study of IL theory and practice. Such data was sought from the database, Web of Science (WoS)[1], plus the contents of two other journals not listed there: the *Journal of Information Literacy* (JIL) and *Communications in Information Literacy* (CIL). By looking for the search term 'information literacy', and removing book reviews, editorial material and other sundries such as letters, meeting abstracts, and corrections, 1,377 papers were retrieved to serve as a representative sample of work in IL. The earliest papers date from 1990, and the latest from December 2012.

Simple bibliometric analyses can be conducted on the dataset. The first, by *disciplinary classification*, follows Stevens (2007). She asked whether IL research was "preaching to the choir" or, conversely, being published outside the LIS presses, thereby disseminating terminology and concepts to a wider audience and helping integrate IL into other academic traditions, as demanded by its advocates (e.g. Breivik and Gee 1989). The aim of the latter would be to introduce its assumptions, terminology, results, and conclusions to other disciplinary areas, permitting these to be criticised and analysed from the perspective of other disciplines. Stevens saw limited evidence of this up to 2007.

The analysis here uses the disciplinary heading assigned to the paper in WoS[2]. Where more than one subject was recorded, the primary heading was used. In table 4.1, some related subjects have been combined for clarity, and papers published since 2010 have been counted separately from those published in 2009 and earlier, permitting judgements about more recent trends.

Library and Information Science remains the most significant discipline, though it has recently declined proportionally. Links exist between LIS practitioners and researchers and computer scientists, with 48.3% of the papers classified primarily as Computer Science being classified secondarily as LIS (though these largely include papers with a relatively technical approach, redolent of Zurkowski's 1974 vision). IL has a growing presence in the field of education and health care/medicine (with the proportionate decline in computer science IL papers partly the result of growth in these other areas). Other fields make little contribution. IL in the business, economics, and management field is largely discussed in conference proceedings, and in linguistics, social science, and communication, each of which could be relevant, very few papers specifically refer to IL. These general observations accord with the conclusions of systematic reviews such as Aharony (2010) and Pinto et al (2010).

Table 4.1   IL literature by disciplinary classification (WoS only)

Classification	2010–12	2009 and previously	All
Business, economics, management	3.1%	1.9%	2.3%
Communication	2.4%	0.6%	1.2%
Computer science	17.9%	23.8%	21.8%
Education & educational research	12.7%	8.4%	9.9%
Engineering, physical sciences, metallurgy, chemistry, biochemistry	3.3%	1.3%	2.0%
Social sciences (incl. human geography, government and law, public administration)	2.1%	0.5%	1.1%
Health care sciences and services, nursing, pharmacy, other clinical & para-clinical disciplines	7.2%	5.1%	5.8%
Information science & library science	50.0%	57.0%	54.6%
Linguistics	1.2%	0.3%	0.6%
Music	0.0%	1.1%	0.7%

The texts were also analysed by *sector*, with each paper classified as either:

- *HE*: IL in higher education (universities, community colleges)
- *K-12*: primary through secondary education
- *Community*: IL in informal learning, community settings, sports clubs, etc.
- *Workplace*: IL amongst employees of an organisation (including teachers, where teachers' own IL is the focus, as opposed to how they teach IL).
- *Public health*: treated separately rather than amalgamated with 'community'. Note that papers dealing with the training of nurses, doctors, or other clinicians were classified as 'HE'; papers in this category were concerned largely with 'health literacy', that is, the information-seeking behaviour of patients and the general public (Frisch et al 2012).
- *Cross-sector*: papers discussing IL in general terms, without a specific sector being identifiable.

A small number of papers (45) can be assigned to more than one category, therefore percentages add up to slightly more than 100.

Proportionally, there has been a recent rise in the number of papers written on IL in the community, and to a less significant extent, K-12 and public health. These sectors, however, remain small in comparison with the papers published on HE. Little has changed since 2002, when Rader reported a similar figure of 60%. These figures are skewed by the CIL and JIL journals, particularly the former. Every one of the 63 papers in the CIL archive was classified as HE, with only two requiring an

Table 4.2   IL literature by sector

Sector	2010–12	2009 and earlier	Total
HE	60.9%	67.0%	64.7%
K-12	11.8%	9.2%	10.2%
Community	7.2%	4.8%	5.7%
Workplace	7.2%	7.2%	7.2%
Public health	7.2%	6.2%	6.6%
Cross-sector	9.1%	9.2%	9.1%

additional sector, one being HE plus K-12, and one HE plus community. JIL's papers were not so singularly focused: nevertheless, 54 of its 75 papers were classified solely as HE, with two more classified as HE plus one other category, amounting to 75%. Even without these two journals, papers with an HE focus outnumbered those in every other category combined.

The growing IL presence in the areas of public health and nursing education has been noted before (Aharony 2010; Wyer and Silva 2009). Growth in 'Evidence Based Medicine' (EBM) or 'Evidence Based Practice' (EBP) is driving this. Wyer and Silva (2009, 893) write that:

> (T)he impetus for something fitting the description of what in 1991 would be dubbed 'evidence-based medicine' was driven by these two related but distinct imperatives: the need to harness and codify the explosion of clinically relevant published research, and the need to develop rubrics for the evaluation of such research that would facilitate literacy and informed consumption on the part of clinicians, and even the lay public.

Wyer and Silva argue, however, that the model of IL at the basis of EBM/EBP is linear, based on instruction (*ibid*). Thus, the relatively successful integration of IL into the clinical and medical professions is based largely on the competency frame. This may explain the antagonistic position that many clinicians continue to adopt towards EBM. As Wyer and Silva say (*ibid*): "It limits the kinds of questions that can be asked and the ways that potential answers found in research literature can be interpreted. It ultimately impedes the ability of EBM, as an instructional method, to fully empower clinicians to be 'evidence literate' within the richness of today's clinical research environment."

This criticism anticipates the third analysis, which considers the *view of IL* in evidence in the dataset. This analysis adopts a pre-existing set of categories: the six frames of information literacy (Bruce et al 2006). Using the six frames in this way has been done before, for example by Andretta (2007a, 7–8). She asked her participants "to identify two of the six statements devised by Bruce et al (2006) to describe the approach to information literacy education adopted by their [HE] institutions". She used the subsequent analysis to support her suggestion (2007, 1) that: "the Content and Competency frames seem to dominate the Higher Education scene at the expense of the remaining four." She also suggested a reason for this (*ibid*): "Such a preference is based on the fact that

Content and Competency frames emphasise, and most importantly assess, types and levels of skills developed by the learners that suit the universities' requirements for 'objective' testing of students' academic performance."

Her conclusions were based on a survey of practitioners at a conference, and thus specifically tied to HE, but I suggest that the six frames can also form the basis of a broader hermeneutic analysis of the research field. It is not necessary to reinvent the wheel, as long as the six frames are not reified: that is, seen as the only possibilities, into which every text must fit. They are used here more for convenience, as a way of organising data, as with Andretta's survey. Additional categories of description may be present. Certainly this is true if the six frames are considered only to be capturing (as they were originally intended to do) the *educational* variation in IL. Nevertheless, even if an educational mission is not explicit, it is still clear in, say, Zurkowski's general attention to the use of particular information banks (which would fall under Bruce et al's content frame) and the skills and competencies required to make best use of these (competency frame). It is also present in Hamelink's Freirean view of literacy, as something which can change social relationships and power structures (thus, Bruce et al's social impact frame). The individual and subjective relationships to information highlighted by Kuhlthau are addressed in the more subjective frames, learning to learn and personal relevance.

Even with such extension, however, the six frames cannot wholly capture the variation in IL research. Limberg et al (2012) stated the importance of sociocultural practice theory to IL: as already noted in this book, the study of IL as practice and transformation may be combined with a study of IL as learning, but should also be considered a separate category of description not captured in Bruce et al's six frames. There are also papers which investigate IL as a theory and/or philosophy in its own right, considering its methodological, epistemological and ontological assumptions, the meaning of terms (including 'IL' itself), and so on. As an example of such a text, the present book is offered. Thus, a total of 8 categories are used in this analysis. These are outlined in table 4.3, along with an indication of the kinds of keywords and concepts which were assigned to the categories (cf. Whitworth 2010).

Around 15% of papers in the dataset were consulted in full in order to assign them to categories: the remainder were assigned through reading the abstract only, which may not be an accurate representation of the full text. In any case, even had I read every paper, my assignations to categories would be open to challenge. However, the intent is not to make declarations about individual papers, but to look for features and

Table 4.3 Categories for analysis

Category	Keywords and concepts
Content	What sources users draw on, directing users to certain sources, copyright, anti-plagiarism, usage of library or other information services
Competency	Skills, instruction, readiness, measuring competency and the effectiveness of instruction, assessment rubrics
Learning to learn	Problem-based learning, enquiry-based learning, metacognition, discipline-specific IL, learning styles, continuing professional development
Personal relevance	Reflection, affective dimensions, sense-making in personal contexts
Social impact	Social inclusion, digital divides, political impact of information or IL, social capital, empowerment
Relational	Phenomenographic approaches, variation, informed learning
Practice	Information practice, organisational issues, decision making, evidence-based practice
Philosophy	Theories of IL, metaliteracy, multimodality

trends in the dataset as a whole. That being the case, the results are presented with an acknowledgement of the inevitability of sampling error, and the percentages in table 4.4 below are advisory, not precise.

Some papers (15 newer (2010–12) and 32 older papers) could not be allocated to a category because investigation revealed that they weren't actually about IL. For example, several papers discussed e-learning techniques with an IL module as a case study, but no contribution was

Table 4.4 Views of IL present in the literature

Category	2010–12	2009 and previously	All
Content	14.0%	17.7%	16.3%
Competency	52.2%	62.6%	58.8%
Learning to learn	18.9%	17.7%	18.1%
Personal relevance	7.2%	5.3%	6.0%
Social impact	8.6%	4.7%	6.1%
Relational	3.1%	2.9%	3.0%
Practice	15.1%	11.1%	12.6%
Philosophy	5.0%	5.6%	5.4%

intended to the IL literature. In a few cases, with older papers, no abstract was present in WoS and the full text could not be tracked down. As with the previous analysis, some papers – in this case a relatively large number (342) – could be assigned to more than one of the eight views of IL: that is, the six derived from Bruce et al's frames of IL, plus IL-as-practice and IL-as-philosophy. For clarity all have been combined in table 4.4.

Considering the dataset as a whole, the domination of competency-based approaches is obvious. However, this category, and the content category, both comprise a smaller proportion of papers published in 2010 and subsequently: significantly so, in the case of competency.

Except for papers dealing with philosophical aspects of IL, which have shown a slight (but not statistically significant) proportional decline, all the other categories registered proportional increases – and, in the case of papers considering the social impact of IL, a significant one.

***

Despite recent signs of change, these analyses support the informal assessment of the field made in chapter 3, and the critique of Tuominen et al (2005, 333), that most texts assume "an individual-centered generic skills definition of IL". The dominance of LIS and the use of this kind of definition go hand in hand (Pawley 2003, 426):

> The language that the LIS community uses to develop the concept of information literacy is, of course, heavily dependent on the traditional style of argument and explanation in the field. Since the prevailing style of LIS discourse uses techno-administrative language to address technical and managerial problems, most professional literature describes applied research into information literacy, provides economic and educational justifications for its existence, and passes on practical tips and recommends methods of evaluation.

This "prevailing style" was present in Zurkowski and Burchinal's views of IL, in Breivik's, and, to a large extent, in Kuhlthau's, though this latter author has a distinctive, subjectivist view of "evaluation". More common is that the evaluation is conducted in accordance with one of two criteria: impact upon student grades (in part the result of so much work focused on HE), and/or rubrics or other measurements of IL that derive from a set of standards, often ACRL but sometimes SCONUL, Big-6 (Eisenberg and Berkowitz 1990), or local organisations (McFarlane 1997, 164).

Standards are rarely *presented* as ends in themselves: as with any other informational resource, there remains scope for different interpretations to emerge. The ACRL standards are student-centred – even Marcum (2002, 11), a critic, says "emphatically" so. Purdue (2003, 654) claims that active citizenship is implied in the ACRL standards, via attention to the ethical use of information. He (*ibid*, 654–5) self-reflects on his own research and information searching process with reference to the ACRL standards and finds himself coming up short on many of them, but notes that standards are "an abstraction... never meant to represent a lock-step process" or something that "one either has or hasn't" (*ibid*, 655–6). Instead, the assessment of IL should be constantly dynamic, evolving, unfinalised – one should learn from mistakes, or where one falls short, and reflect, review, retry, striving to improve but realising there is never a final ideal or end point. The standards can help with this process if considered intellectual resources[3].

Standards also represent a particular *form of thinking*, however; they are cognitive authorities and ways of describing the world. Some, including the ACRL standards and also McFarlane's (1997, 164: see Whitworth 2009, 97–8), strongly imply a linear model of information-seeking. Curl (2001) presents a model, based on one developed for science and engineering disciplines, which is highly linear. She says (2001, 460): "The processes of information production and consumption always begin with an information need".

This cannot be substantiated. Even with active information searches, "needs" are often vaguely stated (cf. Kuhlthau 1993), with searches involving backtracking, iterations, and serendipity (Hepworth and Walton 2009, 52). Moreover, a great deal of information consumption is either passive, with filtering taking place unconsciously or undertaken by third parties, or it takes place in contexts that are much less formalised than that of the 'model' information searcher, a model based mostly around research done into students conducting searches for essays they had to write (Saracevic 2007b; Kuhlthau's work is an example).

Standards also imply *assessment* against the standards; otherwise the standard has no meaning (Inhaber 1976). Thus, these are *cognitive authorities* which encourage the development of instruments of measurement, rubrics, and examinations of some kind (Wilson 1983, 128). These fit well into existing university systems, which are designed to process grades and progression, but that also means other assumptions come into play. For example, Harris claims this is a key reason why the standards describe information literate *individuals* rather than groups or collectives (2008; see also below).

When information behaviour outside the academy or school, and the formalised discourses of assessment, is researched, what is revealed is not linear, individual processes amenable to encapsulation as standards, but messy, iterative, and collective ones. These take place not in the organised space of the library or even the search engine, but in multifaceted landscapes where one cannot assume that all relevant information is, or ever could be, stored in a library or a Zurkowskian 'information bank'. IL must therefore also work on tacit knowledge (Polanyi 1962), orally transmitted, or embodied: e.g. the way to handle a patient, make pizza dough, fight a fire, or handle oneself when faced by a potentially violent situation. Criteria for assessment in these contexts are more informal, based on experience and reflection (Lloyd 2012, 778). Information like this is less likely to be encoded in a written, or at least published[4], text, and more likely to be embedded in communities, in the minds and bodies of other people. Thus, an information literate person must also, at least potentially, recognise other people and their own experience as valid information sources. These are the kinds of *collective* investigations from which practices form.

Thus, Tuominen et al (2005, 336) point out that:

> (T)he most important aspects of IL may be those that cannot be measured at the level of the individual alone... researchers and practitioners have imposed 'invisible constraints' on IL by seeing it as comprised solely of individual cognitive skills.

Such constraints have a long history in LIS research. Saracevic (2007b, 2134–6) notes that studies of information retrieval rarely if ever use more than a single judge per query. Consequently, for systems design, collectives are hard to handle. They are more dialogic, and systems tend towards monologism. Typically, there is inconsistency in how relevance is judged within groups, even where there are procedures designed to secure this agreement. Yet it is also an empirical fact that within collectives, these kinds of judgements are made all the time, and it is in their imperfections that the potential for further learning lies. At the very least, some kind of amalgamation of individual preferences takes place, via a constant dialogue that collectively negotiates differences in interpretation. We *share* insights, and IL must allow for this. The term 'communication' shows this directly; its etymological link with *community* is no coincidence. Both derive from the Latin *communis*, meaning to share, to hold in common.

Yet Harris shows how IL standards pay little attention to the collective (2008, 249):

> The discussion of community is almost completely removed from the IL standards. The only direct mention of community as an influence in information literacy development appears in Standard Four: 'The information literate student, individually or as a member of a group, uses information effectively to accomplish a specific purpose.' The conscious inclusion of 'as a member of a group' in the standard (it is not included in the competency standards or performance indicators to follow) does little to suggest that the group vs. individual situation does not *completely change* the information literacy event in and of itself. It turns the collaborative and social character of the event into an option instead of a requirement of any situation involving communication. Furthermore, placement suggests that it is only in the process of *using* information that groups of individuals, communities, are involved in the information literacy event.

* * *

This argument leads to the conclusion that standards are monologic, and this is a form of thinking that characterises a majority of the published IL literature. IL remains largely driven by categories of description that have been derived from the systems and landscapes of LIS and HE. These have, within IL writ large, created a gap between the idealised, theoretical information user – an individual aware of their information needs and free to make judgements from the full range of information sources – and real information practices, undertaken by individuals (subject to anxiety, pressures of time, cognitive authorities, and other psychological effects), within communities and information landscapes that may help or hinder their experience of variation in different ways.

In essence, this is the same gap as Carr and Kemmis (1986) observed between the idealised educational environment, created by technical means and generic research, and the real-world practices of teachers and students in which these idealisations are applied on the ground, and where they may or may not be validated and found relevant. It is a *theory-practice gap* (*ibid*; also Julien and Williamson 2011). The gap *can* be bridged, and Carr and Kemmis (1986) investigate action research and reflective practice as means by which this can be done, but there exists little empirical work in this area in IL (Lloyd and Williamson 2008; Julien and Williamson 2011; Whitworth 2012). Exhortations that the theory-practice gap be closed will not alone make it happen. If the information landscapes of LIS and HE were conducive to the practices Carr and Kemmis describe, these practices would already be widespread. Why is the gap so persistent? Why have standards, and the competency frame, achieved such a hold over IL despite the richness of variation and collective information behaviour that they neglect to address?

Standards are *products* that, to survive and be accepted as cognitive authorities, must demonstrate they are – or at least, can be perceived as – an improvement over what was there before (older standards, or no standards). Andersen (2006, 215) says that for IL standards to be accepted their proponents must: "make it look as if it is the first time in the history of mankind that a need for a person to be information literate appears." As a result of this perception, standards work to attract resources to those who adhere to the standards. This contributes to the *institutionalisation* of a particular form of IL.

Institutionalisation was Douglas's response (1986) to the question of how "thought styles" reign over "thought worlds": or, in the terminology used here, how cognitive authority is asserted within information landscapes. She shows that institutionalisation is a *cognitive* act, based around how information is validated and knowledge is formed. Chapter 1 already demonstrated that social institutions and individual thinking are dependent upon one another (Douglas 1986, 45). But whereas some communities are transient, even momentary (a 'community' of pedestrians can gather and be of sufficient shared purpose to create a collective practice – make the cars stop so all community members can cross a road – but then disappear again seconds later), institutions have a stability about them that (*ibid*, 46) "needs a parallel cognitive convention to sustain..." These cognitive conventions become embedded into the organisations, systems, technologies, routines, and habits that sustain the institution, shaping what is considered valid in that institution and what is not, and thus controlling and deflecting uncertainty (*ibid*, 48):

> Past experience is encapsulated in an institution's rules so that it acts as a guide to what to expect from the future. The more fully the institutions encode expectations, the more they put uncertainty under control, with the further effect that behaviour tends to conform to the institutional matrix: if this degree of coordination is achieved, disorder and confusion disappear. Schotter presents institutions as entropy-minimizing devices. They start with rules of thumb and norms; eventually they can end by storing all the useful information. When everything is institutionalized, no history or other storage devices are necessary: "The institution tells all" (Schotter 1981, 139).

Douglas acknowledges that what is missing from this analysis is the question of how institutions get started, how they "get enough stability to do all of that" (*ibid*). She seeks an explanation in how institutions provide ways for individuals to establish sameness and difference. Thus, institutions allow individuals to save cognitive work, something that cognitive science has shown we are innately inclined to do (see Blaug 2007, 28*ff*). Institutions provide classificatory schemes, patterns, and acts of remembering, rooted in habits and routines but also validated by interactions with other members of the institutionalised community, who are constantly confirming them by their own adherence to these habits and routines. Thus, cognitive authority becomes invested in the institution as a whole. Challenges to these institutionalised values will be looked upon as eccentric at best, at worst subversive, possibly illegal (consider how challenges to the institution of heterosexuality are treated around the world).

Institutions can facilitate the formation of knowledge, as well as constrain it. The "labels" they provide "stabilise the flux of social life" (*ibid*, 100). We need to draw on such pre-existing ways of thinking to do anything at all. If we could not we would need to start each day from first principles; there would be no continuity to our existence[5]. Yet institutions become institutions by also, to some extent, creating "the realities to which they apply" (*ibid*). Institutions routinise practice, keeping it within an established structure, a standard operating procedure (March, Olsen and Christensen 1979, 140–1); Bourdieu (1977) has called this routinisation *habitus*. Stakeholders within any institution that conform to the habitus develop *capital* therein: this allows them to attract resources from the institution, reinforcing their position (and the institution's), through the "Matthew effect"; "to those that hath shall be given" (March et al 1979, 152). Institutions (Douglas 1986, 92):

> (S)ystematically direct individual memory and channel our perceptions into forms compatible with the relations they authorise. They fix processes that are essentially dynamic, they hide their influence, and they rouse our emotions to a standardised pitch on standardised issues. Add to all this that they endow themselves with rightness and send their mutual corroboration cascading through all the levels of our information system... the hope of intellectual independence is to resist, and the necessary first step in resistance is to discover how the intellectual grip is laid upon our mind.

This is not easy, for what Douglas is describing are procedures that are akin to Gramsci's notion of hegemony (*ibid*, 99):

To analyse our own collective representations, we should relate what is shared in our mental furnishing to our common experience of authority and work. To know how to resist the classifying pressures of our institutions, we would like to start an independent classificatory exercise. Unfortunately, all the classifications that we have for thinking with are provided ready-made, along with our social life. For thinking about society we have at hand the categories we use as members of society speaking to each other about ourselves.

Yet counterhegemonic activity is possible. Critiques of an institution that are based on the validity claims of that institution are valid critiques by definition. If new classifications are produced – new experiences of variation, ways of thinking and learning that challenge institutionalised ones – then an institution can change, even fall. Institutions, at least in the persistent sense that Douglas means, do not constitute the entirety of our information-processing infrastructure, and many institutions are in tension and contradict with each other.

Thus, conditions can be *consciously* created in which the institution is scrutinised. Institutions govern our thinking, yes, but not *deterministically* – that is, shaping all possibilities, forever. If such a realm existed then 'freedom' would merely mean a choice between pre-filtered alternatives. But institutions are part of the landscapes within which we can develop our own interpretations of the world and, as a result of this learning, transform it. 'Learning' is not about selecting something from a limited range of options, but is a process of self-discovery; not being told something is important, but coming for oneself to conceive its importance, its relevance, to one's own life. This can only be done through practice that is in turn based on learning, and a type of learning that goes beneath the surface content of a discipline and embraces deeper methods such as self-reflection, action research, and critical thinking.

There is a need, in short, to bridge the theory-practice gap, and these are methods that have already been shown to do just that. The question is not what the methods are, nor whether the gap needs in fact to be closed, but whether the institutionalisation of IL in the LIS and HE sectors will permit these matters to be addressed.

* * *

A *critical* study of the IL literature must now draw attention to the inequalities that exist: that is, the field's 'lumpiness'. The shape of the field is the result not of random fluctuations, but evidence of structures in the landscape which shape the experience of variation therein. Particular IL discourses have become institutionalised. Although there have been contributions from studies of, say, the social impact of information, constructivist workplace IL pedagogies, and so on, it remains the professional contexts of librarians and other LIS practitioners, higher education, and standards and competencies that are driving, not so much definitions of the IL field, but its *perception*. These are what IL has institutionalised itself around.

Weiner (2012) discusses the institutionalising of IL as a positive thing, using the term as a way to describe IL's integration across HE curricula. But Weiner's paper is clearly focused on HE: it defines IL in the first paragraph (*ibid*, 287) as the ACRL standards, it says on the next page (*ibid*, 288) that "[f]rom the time that Zurkowski named the concept of information literacy... librarians have sought ways to integrate it into learning in institutions of higher education", and implicitly – via the first line of the section "Differences in Institutions in Higher Education" which invokes only the US – it is country-specific. Therefore, for all that her insights have value when seeking an understanding of how the organisational structure in HE blocks the integration of IL, it seems fair to claim that this paper is an example of institutionalisation in the more negative sense as well. It draws on context-specific ways of thinking, and generalises them to the whole field.

The "Matthew effect" of institutionalisation is the significant driver: the perceived need to attract attention, and thus resources, to support the library's role in addressing issues raised by *A Nation at Risk*. McCrank (1991, 42) stated that the ALA/Breivik agenda was "part of librarianship's angry reaction" to their omission from that report. As noted, IL was defined as the added value the library could offer higher education institutions, and once the standards were formulated in order to express this outcome in terms which meshed with accreditation regimes, IL's institutionalisation became tangible. As Pawley (2003, 424) notes: "Ownership of so politically charged a term assigns rights and privileges. It provides justification for resources, including staff, equipment, and research grants and funds for program development."

A contradiction, however, is that while an institution can work well to attract resources from *certain* sources, it may simultaneously be less effective at attracting resources (capital) from *other* pools, even when the institution may be based partly around the belief that these other pools help support it. This is certainly true of IL, which regularly reiterates the importance of alliances between library educators, academics, and managers when seeking to integrate IL into curricula and campus-wide policy. The lack of such integration is a long standing complaint. Breivik was clear (1986, 47) that "information gathering and evaluation skills must be... learned within existing departments... rather than in stand-alone bibliographic instruction programs", and (1991, 256) that the *Final Report* "was not written for librarians or to justify library use". Yet, justified though the criticism is, to be still hearing it from, e.g., Badke (2012) means that explanations need to be sought elsewhere than the fact that the complaint has simply not been heard. From a library perspective it makes *professional* sense to promote IL and try to integrate it throughout its local context (the HE institution). Librarianship as a discipline is based around the tenets of LIS, so spreading IL through a local context aims at further optimising the performance of the university's information system. Spreading IL through a network of alliances, based around this institutionalised value, also makes *organisational* sense, as success at this task would raise the capital of the library. Nevertheless, if IL can be perceived, even by its sympathisers, as "an effort to deny the ancillary status of librarianship by inventing a social malady with which librarians as 'information professionals' are uniquely qualified to deal" (Foster 1993, 344), one needs to look more deeply at reasons why the hoped-for integration has not taken place.

There are two ways of reshaping the query. First, one could ask: is it that IL is not being taught outside the library/HE; or, rather, are librarians and those who write about IL from within this landscape unable to perceive the work that is going on outside their purview, even if those undertaking it are not calling it 'IL'?

Second, what is it about the way the library generates and validates knowledge that is holding open the gap between IL theory – which, more and more, is based on the notion that IL permeates all communicative exchanges, is dialogic, multifaceted, and rooted both in personal psychology and collective decision-making processes – and IL practice, which, at best, struggles to accommodate this view, and at worst, actively represses it in favour of a monologic, technical, standards-based approach?

Can libraries/LIS give up information literacy, or at least, recognise that it is a notion that spreads well beyond their own landscape – even if this would *strengthen,* not weaken their position? Institutionalisation makes this difficult, and it is more insidious for often going unnoticed. A typically frustrated article here came from Kempcke (2002). It serves as an example of how institutionalisation can seep into discourse, manifested as an unscrutinised belief that the library is *innately* the best place for IL education. Kempcke starts by saying that for librarians to be effective in initating information literacy or other educational reforms on campus, "they must be seen not only as equals [by faculty], but leaders in higher education, as scholars skilled in teaching, and as vital participants in the governance of their institutions" (*ibid*, 531). He aggressively bemoans the condescension manifested towards librarians' teaching credentials, librarians' limited view of their own professionalism, and the consequent ghettoisation of IL. Militaristic metaphors abound, from the title of the piece (which invokes Sun Tzu's *Art of War*) to his talk of "battles" and suggestion that "war may be inevitable if we are not being granted the position in the organizational culture we deserve" (*ibid*, 538). Librarians are described as a "higher stratum [than faculty], ready and willing to sweep down with comprehensive and awe-inspiring assistance. We are formidable and skilled warriors against the forces of ignorance" (*ibid*, 541).

Yet what does Kempcke seek? The development of IL in students, or the boosting of librarians' capital within the university? This passage suggests the latter – or at least, that the former is the route through which the latter will be achieved: "[a]s our influence increases, the direct and indirect benefits to the academic library also increase. The more we skillfully and successfully address the critical problems (such as information illiteracy) facing our campuses, the more likely we are to gain prestige and attract an appropriate distribution of resources" (*ibid*, 544). Nevertheless, he is right to recognise that "[t]he ACRL Standards are only a weapon that we can use to win the larger IL war. They are not a victory in and of themselves" (*ibid*, 532). Thus, his claim that integration will benefit all is not based on a belief that the standards *per se* should come to govern any working (or learning) practices outside their original context, the library. He appreciates that librarians need to better "comprehend the organizational culture in which we work", and focus continuing professional development (CPD) efforts on developing this understanding, for: "[t]here is no article that can tell you how to do it because no author can understand the political climate at every campus. Though there may be similarities, each program needs to be customized to the existing institutional culture" (*ibid*, 545).

Thus, despite his warlike metaphors, Kempcke is right to recognise that work to integrate IL onto any particular campus – a specific context – requires an understanding of that context, and not merely generic claims about what IL 'should be'. Yet the way he presents his case simultaneously depends on an institutionalised, and unscrutinised, belief that only in the library can there be 'real' IL; IL that meets certain criteria or standards. But as already asked – what if there already *is* IL going on, quite healthily, outside this context? What if the reasons why there is no integration come about because the two 'sides', facing each other across the gap, have not *learned to see* the practices of the other – thus, are not experiencing the full variation of the phenomenon?

Leckie and Fullerton (1999) analyse the different "pedagogical discourses" of librarians and faculty. They, like many others, call for greater integration of IL but recognise that (*ibid*, 1): "numerous studies have shown that academic librarians and faculty do not understand each other's roles or expectations very well". Julien and Pecoskie (2009) also describe differing perceptions of role. Their librarian research subjects did not view teaching faculty as their clientele, focusing instead on students. Librarians had a sense of deference towards faculty, seeing faculty giving time as a "gift", with no reciprocity expected, as revealed by phrases such as faculty "allowing" librarians time to come into their courses, for example. Yet they remain unable to suggest ways out of this unequal relationship beyond just asserting that the relationship needs to equalise. In the conclusion (Julien and Pecoskie 2009, 153) they say: "As in all power relationships, it undoubtedly falls to the lower-status members in those relationships (i.e., librarians) to seek redress. Since teaching faculty value subject expertise primarily, it is proposed that redress be grounded in librarians' demonstrations of their expertise." But this will offer no challenge to existing institutionalised perceptions of role and context, despite the fact that, as McCrank noted more than twenty years ago now (1991, 423): "The paradox of information literacy is that it calls upon librarians to change more than users", yet (Elmborg 2006, 193), these issues raise "important fundamental questions about libraries and their inability to challenge their own historical definitions of who they are and why they define their work as they do."

* * *

The lack of integration and the consequent isolation of IL in the academic library are based, ultimately, on a fundamental misunderstanding, but believing that this misunderstanding concerns the question of where IL should be located and who should teach it, is itself a misunderstanding. In fact, the question that has not been properly answered is *what information literacy is, and what its underlying theories should be*. The library-, HE-, and competency-based paradigm of IL accords very well with the technical, LIS-basis of IL, as developed so influentially by Zurkowski, Burchinal, Demo, and Breivik. But as Kuhlthau, Bruce, and others have shown, even within this broader *educational* paradigm of IL – seeing the information literate individual *or* community as something which can be nurtured through developing a broad understanding of learning processes – LIS can only take us so far. Additional theoretical contributions are required from, at least, PCP and phenomenography: these realms help us understand the dialogic interplay between the subjective and intersubjective realms when it comes to making judgements about information, the role of uncertainty and emotion, and how to make the sort of collective judgements that are very difficult, if not impossible, to capture in an information system (Saracevic 2007b). But even this expanded theoretical base, as part 1 has shown, cannot successfully handle issues of *authority*: how the experience of variation, itself a process of selecting between an essentially infinite number of possibilities, can be *governed* in various ways.

This was the insight that Hamelink brought to IL, which the other authors mentioned so far have, on the whole, left largely implicit: it comes out most strongly in certain chapters of *Informed Learning* (Bruce 2008, particularly 107–132), and even in that work there is no explicit discussion of the role of power and hegemony. To fulfil the vision of Hamelink, and reclaim the political heart of IL, one must do more than simply learn about an information landscape: one must *transform* it, build one's own, and this will require practices that cannot be captured by a strictly educational approach.

This is – emphatically – not arguing that libraries should cease to play a role in the teaching, development, and definition of IL. On the contrary, there is far too much necessary expertise in the sector to dismiss its contributions, whether now or previously. However (Elmborg 2002):

> In order to provide a working definition of information literacy, we must navigate two competing visions of the library. In one vision, the library retains its status as neutral purveyor of information, and information literacy is based on students mastering the libraries' tools and systems. In this vision, information literacy is reduced to mastering a set of library skills with traditional tools. In the other more ambitious vision, the library becomes a site for student empowerment, a place where students create genuine questions and construct their own answers. In this vision, the library's role in perpetuating disciplinary classifications and organizing and disseminating authoritative knowledge becomes part of what students must understand to be information literate, but only part.

In a different paper, Elmborg, like Hamelink, invokes Freirean notions of education and literacy (2006, 193), asking:

> What is the role of the library in the Freirean vision of critical literacy? Is the library a passive information bank where students and faculty make knowledge deposits and withdrawals, or is it a place where students actively engage existing knowledge and shape it to their own current and future uses? And what is the librarian's role as an educator in this process?

Elmborg claims (*ibid*, 193–4) that the lack of attention to schools' role as "shapers of student consciousness" is a consequence of the LIS research paradigm, which like other essentially technical subjects, *decontextualises* phenomena and thus separates students "from social and economic contexts". This is firmly linked to the positivistic approach to science, oriented to prediction and generalised 'best practice' (cf. Carr and Kemmis 1986, particularly 51–81). Positivism is a way of thinking – an epistemology – that seeks explanations of events in order that their underlying laws can be discovered, so future events of that type can be predicted and, the implication goes, controlled: "On the basis of these predictions it becomes possible, by manipulating a particular set of variables, to control events so that desirable goals are acheived and undesirable consequences eliminated" (Carr and Kemmis 1986, 67). But once all human activity is seen as essentially context-dependent, that latter phrase prompts the question: desirable to whom? Whose goals are driving the positivistic enquiry? Such questions are seen as irrelevant in positivism, but they are essential to information literacy. Hence, the insufficiency of the LIS paradigm when it comes to understanding real information landscapes.

The politics at the heart of Hamelink's vision of IL was not based around the notion that the information literate person has learned to fit themselves and their enquiries into an existing information system. Rather, it is based on self-development: raising awareness of the value of one's own culture, history, and associated stock of information, and developing one's own ways of processing them. It is about increasing "communicative competence in the information age" (Whitworth 2007), enabling students to become more informed and breaking away from the instrumental "template" of IS- and standards-based approaches (Thornton 2010), and similar work called for by Kapitzke (2003). It attends to all forms of information and the relevant skills and awareness needed to process these forms. Often, this information not only is not accessible through a library or search engine, but never will be, being embodied in the practices, values, and even movements of colleagues or companions. This sort of knowledge – orally transmitted, practical, encoded in a minority language or slang, in the form of imagery, etc. – may often be more relevant to disempowered populations, whether in the developing (Dorner and Gorman 2011) or developed world (Bruce and Bishop 2008). In fact, precisely because it cannot be digitised, this is why the "digital divide" opens up along this fault line.

In the end, the problem may not be just IL's institutionalisation in the academic library, but in *academic culture* itself. Lamenting the lack of collaboration between librarians and academics therefore misses the point: this is why the continued concentration on HE, little changed since Rader's 2002 assessment, is so damaging. Elmborg (2006, 197) says that:

> While all communities rank literacy performance to some extent, academia is relatively unique in its formal and ritualized assessments, with the result that in academia 'nearly everything is graded in more or less subtle ways' [Becher and Trowler 1989, 81]. Through *institutionalized* processes [emphasis added] – such as assigning grades to students, granting tenure and promotion, conducting peer review of books and articles, establishing institutional rankings, and the ranking of publications for prestige – judgments about quality permeate higher education.

But a university education is very far from being the only learning experience that a normal human being will have in their lives. If IL is to be understood *dialogically*, the consequences of this simple and obvious fact must be understood. And as noted, instead of just continuing to assert the need for change, IL as an academic field of study needs itself to fundamentally change. If a theory-practice gap exists – and in IL, it clearly does – then one way to close it is to retheorise the field around the need to close it, directly addressing the links between the formation of knowledge, learning, practice, transformation, and authority. That is the task of part 2 of this book.

Notes

1. The WoS search was undertaken, and the results tabulated, by Stephen Pearson of the University of Manchester library, to whom thanks are again due.
2. The JIL and CIL papers are therefore not included in this analysis. Bearing in mind these are LIS journals, their inclusion would in fact reinforce the bias seen here.
3. Media literacy educators in the US have also promoted a set of core principles for their discipline (Domine 2011, 447–8). See also *http://crln.acrl.org/content/72/7/420.full* – standards for IL specifically directed at teacher education in the US.
4. It could potentially be found in a personal diary, an email, a notebook, etc, but though these are written texts, one would be unlikely to find them in a library unless they were archive material.
5. As, for instance, experienced by Guy Pearce's character in the movie *Memento*.

Part 2: Reconstructing IL

"Anyone can cook."

Chef Gusteau, *Ratatouille* [dir: Brad Bird]

Colonising IL

Abstract: This chapter begins the process of enquiring more deeply into the nature of cognitive authority, and its influence on IL.. Learning about authority, and understanding the ways in which it can be wielded both to make change, and retard it, is key to transforming practice in any social context. First, the theories of Jürgen Habermas are outlined, as his work offers a very useful framework for distinguishing between forms of rationality and, thus, how both dialogic and monologic approaches, ideally, should combine in a broad view of authority, but in practice are out of balance in the institutions of modernity. However, Habermas's theories cannot form the only pillar of a radical IL, because he is guilty of over-abstraction, and insufficiently attentive to the nature of democracy as a real, lived experience.

Key Words: Critical theory, Habermas, colonisation, organisations, counterpublics, hierarchism, vigilance

Part 1 critiqued IL from the perspective of dialogism, concluding that it has become institutionalised around a limited, monologic view of the broad range of interactions and practices which constitute work with information. Part 2 will respond to this critique, but must avoid falling into the trap of asserting that the closing of IL's theory-practice gap will come about simply by calling for its closure. Where resistance to change is pervasive, repeating calls for change is counter-productive unless one investigates the nature and source of the resistance.

Part 2 will undertake this investigation, enquiring into the role of *authority* in information exchange, and through doing so, synthesising IL's educational, learning-based aspects with its practical, transformational ones. Understanding why the theory-practice gap remains open requires an understanding of power and politics, and how these both facilitate and retard change in particular contexts. As Easterby-Smith et al lamented (1998, 262), work on organisational learning and transformation tends to consider power as a limiting factor, something that blocks the creation of a learning organisation. Instead, political factors need to be integrated into theories of learning, including IL. And because political questions – whose goals, whose definitions, which cognitive authorities are shaping the information landscape – are context-specific, and must be investigated and interpreted anew in each landscape, any theoretical investigation of power must also contribute to an innately *practical* understanding of how information landscapes are shaped by authorities within each setting. Learning about authority, and understanding the ways in which it can be wielded, both to make change and retard it, is key to transforming practice in any social context. Therefore, this learning about authority, about how it is assigned and distributed within information landscapes, and if necessary transformed, is the central pillar of radical IL. I suggest that the lack of such a theory is the reason Hamelink's Freirean notion of IL has been mostly neglected.

This theory of IL has three main elements, explored in chapters 5, 6, and 7. First, the critical theories of Jürgen Habermas will be outlined. These provide a strong foundation for studies of social change, and are particularly attuned to the role of communication therein. However, over-abstraction prevents Habermas's theories from fully constituting a radical IL due to their lacking practical and contextualisable elements. IL can be more fully explored using the theories of Mikhail Bakhtin, which are firmly rooted in everyday, prosaic communication (Morson and Emerson 1990) and directly consider the nature of cognitive authority. Bakhtin's ideas, which have not previously been applied to IL in any detailed way, are investigated in chapter 6. Chapter 7 then returns to the field of IL-as-practice and synthesises it with learning-based approaches by developing the methodological link between practice and phenomenography.

* * *

The study of power requires the selection of a path between contrasting tendencies: the problem of "how to make holistic structures or systems weak enough to permit agency and reflection, and yet also strong enough to avoid an idealistic underestimation of their constitutive efficacy and resistance to efforts to change them" (Bohman 1989, 385). Work in IL has tended to underestimate the strength of existing structures in this way, leading to frustration manifested in repeated exhortations for change. On the other hand, critical theories, which previously investigated power and its role in limiting access to information and meaning, have sometimes gone to the other extreme, and found no way through the barriers which emerge. Marcuse (1964), for example, described the deadening effect of the mass media on popular culture and anticipated some of Hamelink's criticisms of the use of these media to control thought and desire. But neither he, nor fellow Frankfurt School theorists Horkheimer and Adorno (1972), found ways to address these pathologies without collapsing into irrational forms of self-expression such as love or anger (Habermas 1984, 382). What they lacked was an effective *agency* of change.

One cannot just declare that existing ways of teaching and practicing IL are inadequate. One must also accept that they structure activity regardless and thus, like any institutionalised practice, form an environment that will, at best, be unsupportive of efforts to change it, and may well actively block them. Any attempt to transform practice must therefore understand why and how that practice has become structured in these ways. Nevertheless, through processes of learning and transformation, change in these practices is *possible* despite structural biases lined up against it.

The theories of Habermas, though inspired by the work of the Frankfurt School, offer greater potential here than his antecedents (see also Whitworth 2007; 2009). However, one must also attend to their limits. A well-developed criticism is that of Blaug (1999a), who suggests that Habermas is too abstract and generic to assist with the design of actual, democratic social structures. Habermas's theories allow a distinction to be made between an institutionalised IL and more radical forms, as his work can show how systems of information exchange, including educational practices, can be constructed in ways that retard learning, regardless of rhetoric to the contrary. But he is insufficiently aware of democracy as rooted in real, everyday practices and lived experiences. Consequently, his work can constitute one pillar of radical IL, but cannot fully elucidate it.

The most fundamentally relevant aspect of Habermas's work to IL comes with his exploration of alternate forms of rationality, and how these form valid bases for decisions and the communicative acts, the sharing and exchange of information, on which such decisions are based. In this exploration, Habermas sought a way out of the blockages reached by the Frankfurt School. Those critical theorists saw no agent of change as, for them, only one type of rationality was empirically significant: instrumentality, the fulfilling of goals. An instrumentally-rational decision is one that helps move an individual, group, or organisation towards the successful fulfilment of a predetermined goal. Such decisions tend to be based on information processing that gathers the necessary information, filters it for relevance and credibility, analyses it to assess costs and benefits, and is procedurally firm (Morgan 1999, 11*ff*). But instrumental rationality is also convergent, usually seeking the "one best" way to proceed. In its 'pure' form it is inflexible, because "when new problems arise they are often ignored because there are no ready made responses... standardised procedures and channels of communication" (*ibid*, 29). Instrumental rationality, in short, tends toward monologism, and is based on considerations to which competency-based approaches to IL are well suited.

This is not meant to dismiss the value of such cognitive work. Instrumental considerations like these are clearly important in decision-making and, without such work, decisions would risk being based on counterknowledge (Thompson 2008). However, Habermas also defined rationality as "an emergent property of forms of human life and communication" (Outhwaite 1996, 116). He sought to explore *intersubjective* forms of rationality, where the claim that something is 'rational', and thus justifiable, cannot be made by any one subject acting alone, even with reference to objective considerations such as scientific insights. Habermas terms this *communicative rationality*.

Rationality inheres in communication because any speech act raises *validity claims* that can be criticised and defended (Habermas 1984, 8–10). Habermas believes that, through a process of freely raising, criticizing, and defending claims, actors in any communicative space can approach the ideal end-point of rational communication: that is, the reaching of a consensus (*ibid*, 11). Rationality is manifested in the conscious agreement of multiple subjects acting autonomously but interdependently, drawing on the information available to them and coming together in discussion to jointly establish ways forward. To be communicatively rational, these situations must conform to certain ideals (McCarthy 1984, 306–7):

- the supposition that consensus is possible and can be distinguished from false consensus;
- decisions have been taken with reference to the force of the better argument rather than accidental or systematic constraints on communication;
- all participants have an equal chance to put forward, question, ground or refute any statement.

These conditions are met in what Habermas calls the ideal speech situation (ISS). Thus, "rationality can be measured by the degree of openness or closure in communication... [and] the goals of truth, freedom and justice are not mere utopian dreams, but are anticipated in ordinary communication..." (Ray 1993, 26–7). Habermas has here been criticised (e.g. Lyotard 1984) for imposing normative standards on democratic debate in a contradictory way, but as its name indicates, the ISS must be seen as an *ideal*. Ideals are philosophical constructs against which real situations can be judged, "centres of gravitation" (Wellmer 1985, 61) to which actors can aspire. Communicatively rational decision-making is not a fixed set of practices that can be imposed upon the messiness of real interactions, by external interests. Instead, it is a process of continual checking and adjustment of practice against the ideal, *by members of the forum*.

Habermas does not discount the value of instrumental rationality, and the forms of knowledge it produces. Both rationalities potentially contribute to learning and transformation in ways that are, ideally, complementary and in balance in any given social space. Without action oriented towards reaching a goal rather than reaching an understanding, decision-making, or indeed any organisational activity, would become mired in endless discussion. However, Habermas analyses how modern society has inexorably valorised instrumental rationality over communicative. Those aspects of the social structure designed to promote communicative rationality – that is, autonomous, context-specific learning, and subsequent transformation – are becoming subservient to technical forms of control over practice. Modern societies therefore have a "distorted understanding of rationality" (Habermas 1984, 66), which promotes certain *forms of thinking* over others. The de-skilling of the mass of professional workers, and the spread of installations for the monitoring of human behaviour (up to and including mass surveillance), are part of this general tendency. The generation and analysis of data is important for making rational, instrumental decisions, but the modern scale of it has resulted in the creation of information banks that surpass any human scale of understanding. Instrumental rationality works also on the structures of language itself, restricting the meanings of words and other packets of information in monologic ways. Language, information systems, and anything else with informative potential, become, at least potentially, instruments through which dominant interests can fulfil goals regardless of any communicative processes which scrutinise and thus validate these ends or means.

Habermas's early term for these processes appeared in the title of his first major work *The Structural Transformation of the Public Sphere* (1989, but first published in German in 1962). Later (1984; 1987), he talked about the "colonisation of the lifeworld". While the latter is a much more theoretically sophisticated notion, their essential core is shared: the transformation of communicative spaces from egalitarian fora, in which new ideas could be freely explored, into media that are harder to access, controlled, and largely wielded by dominant interests in society. As Outhwaite writes, "critical assessment of public policy in rational discussion, oriented to a concept of the public interest" – in other words, public scrutiny of decisions and validity claims – is transformed into "a manipulated public sphere in which states and corporations use 'publicity' in the modern sense of the word to secure for themselves a kind of plebiscitary acclamation" (Outhwaite 1996, 7). Under conditions of colonisation, information is less likely to be intersubjectively validated by those affected by it (Habermas 1984, 358). Society becomes steered, not by public debate, but by money and power, which come to substitute for these (Habermas 1984, 342; 1987, 180–5). As Hamelink recognised, the broadcast media play a significant role here, as do the legal profession, public relations firms, political consultants, and so on. Within organisations, operations and sanctions such as the withdrawal of resources, or encouragement in the form of reward and promotion structures, seek *instrumentally* to ensure that the goals of dominant (capital-holding) stakeholders within the organisation are met, regardless of the impact on subordinates, and regardless of their ways of learning and thinking about practice and the environment they inhabit.

Habermas's theories therefore demonstrate a specific concern with how intersubjective dialogue is devalued in organisational decision-making and, in a preliminary way, help us perceive structural biases in our knowledge-forming systems. His theories hold relevance for IL because they attend to "the social organization of documents and knowledge in society" (Andersen 2006, 219), and how this is transformed from a more *communicative, distributed* authority to a more *instrumental, centralised* authority[1]. The lifeworld is not a neutral medium through which communication is transmitted. Instead, the lifeworld, and all its component information landscapes, are structures that have been built over time, significantly shaped by dominant interests (whether in society or in particular local contexts). These structures determine what can be communicated, to whom, and how (Andersen 2006, 220). When we study information exchange through such a lens, we are therefore obliged to notice that communication and information production (Andersen 2008, 359):

> (A)re carried out for a reason. They accomplish a human communicative purpose that is a part of the organization's social division of labor, its social organization, developed historically.... It should follow from this statement that insofar as 'texts help organize social activities and social structure,' (Bazerman 1988, p. 10), those activities that organize texts for retrieval and documentation are indirectly involved in organizing social activities and social structure. Thus, knowledge organization both supports and transforms social structure.

Within organisations, information behaviour is more intensely colonised, because the structures of information exchange and knowledge development – and the potential sanctions for breaking them – are more rigorous and formalised than within less structured entities such as small groups or networks (though communities can still assert powerful sanctions, such as ridicule or exclusion). Job descriptions, formal procedures, requirements to use particular computer systems to process information, all mean that actors in many organisations "act communicatively only *with reservation*. They know they *can* have recourse to formal regulations, not only in exceptional but in routine cases; there is no *necessity* for achieving consensus by communicative means..." (Habermas 1987, 310, but see also Klein and Truex 1996, and below). Thus, the colonised organisation becomes decoupled from the communicative structures of society, in which its activities can be validated by a wider spectrum of people (Habermas 1987, 145–8). Decisions become taken with reference to, and eventually organised around, instrumental criteria, set and judged only by 'experts' in whatever field is under scrutiny. Office holders become subject to formal rules, ways of influencing practice, of making decisions about information, and discouraged from stepping outside the 'territory' of their role, making it harder to engage in a dialogue with the diversity of viewpoints and perspectives needed to reach a consensus (*ibid*, 355).

Instrumental forms of knowledge-processing deliver efficiency gains. However, these come at the price of the scrutiny of decisions taken. One of the dynamics which distinguishes organsations and organisational types from each other (see Mintzberg 1989) hinges around how much debate, autonomy, and creativity is permitted to flourish within an organisation. These are crucial processes in double-loop learning, the questioning of basic assumptions, but organisations also work to channel them into the more effective fulfilment of predetermined, instrumental goals (single-loop learning). Although both these are important within organisational decision making, *trade-offs* exist between them. When should the claims of a hierarchy, on which its position may be based, be opened up for review? When should debate stop and action start, and who should take responsibility for it? As asked at the end of chapter 1: what are the *cognitive costs of hierarchy* (Blaug 2007; 2010) – and are these worth paying in particular contexts at particular times? The question of how a community can maintain *vigilance* over the trade-offs it faces vis-à-vis decision making is key to whether colonisation can be *treated as a learning opportunity*, rather than as a restriction on learning.

To see colonisation as a learning opportunity requires that its operations must be understood by actors within organisations who may wish to decolonise (and thus transform) these organisations. To reveal colonisation is not always easy. Hegemony involves, at least in part, constructing an environment in which control and externalised authority seem natural, with the opposite – autonomous, empowering, and inclusive activity – treated with suspicion. Assumptions that "to act together successfully in the world necessarily entails a hierarchy of command, centralised control... the institutionalisation of roles of expertise and leadership... the division of labour, the systematisation of tasks and the immunisation of elite decision-makers against input from those defined as lacking expertise" (Blaug 1999b, 35) combine into a *paradigm*, an unscrutinised (institutionalised) belief that Blaug calls "hierarchism". The paradigm of hierarchism is self-sustaining in various ways. Without adequate theories, and with communicative forms of decision-making typically devalued (Blaug 1999b), those seeking to learn about alternative organisational forms lack resources on which to base their efforts for transformation. In other words, their information landscape is unsupportive of this enquiry.

Meyer and Rowan (1991, 53) describe "institutional isomorphism" as the tendency, over time, for institutions in the same domain to become more alike. This reinforces hierarchies, by attracting resources through the 'Matthew effect'. Organisations that adopt culturally acceptable forms, and provide information (like accounts) demanded by resource-providers or legal protectorates, acquire legitimacy and can elicit resources from other organisations as a result (DiMaggio and Powell

1983, Friedland and Alford 1991). "Anti-organisations", or those with mission statements or structures that do not accord with hierarchism, struggle to acquire the same legitimacy. For example, consider the restrictions placed on access to research grants. A community organisation seeking to contribute in this way to the collective learning processes of society would likely find it difficult to acquire funds to support such work without subordinating itself to a formally constituted HE or R & D institution. Access to resources is thereby limited by instrumental assumptions about what "research" is and who is best placed to undertake it, as Carr and Kemmis (1986) point out.

Thus, paradigms of hierarchism contribute to the institutionalisation of instrumental organisational forms and, once institutionalisation is under way, information practices within the organisation become oriented towards sustaining existing sources of legitimacy to keep resources flowing. If problems and uncertainties arise, institutionalisation pressures the organisation to seek to deal with them within the forms, structures, and value systems that it already has (Di Maggio and Powell 1983). Thus, the sociotechnical systems within the organisation – including information technologies, procedures, and the socialisation of recruits (Turner 1971) – are evaluated, and thus designed, with increasingly objective and generic criteria in mind, rather than elements that permit democratic scrutiny, review, and transformation of these criteria by those who work with and are affected by the systems.

Hierarchism does not erase communicative rationality from organisations. Klein and Truex (1996, 253) observed communicative actions and reciprocal information exchanges dominating within meetings, concluding that over 80% of exchanges could be considered communicative rather than instrumental. Within the meetings they observed, the aim of participants was to achieve consensus and a mutual understanding of the issue under discussion. Where instrumental action was observed, it involved organising and supervising work that resulted from these decisions. Thus, the communicative actions helped the group interpret the environment and reach an understanding, but were, alone, insufficient for transformation. Without these communicative actions, however, the subsequent instrumental action would either have never taken place, or would have been less adequate, possibly irrational. Instrumental actions therefore do not *have* to originate from objective and generic criteria: nor, indeed, from the subjective whims of a leader. The authority to engage in a particular course of action *can* be intersubjectively invested in a collective. This is, in the end, the democratic ideal.

Yet colonisation also works by devaluing communicatively-rational processes in particular contexts. Is the intersubjective view permitted to override the objective (or, in a monarchy, the subjective) authority? Who is *permitted* to address a problem? Whose learning will be attended to, and how? Whose purposes are served by a learning process? Hierarchism promotes 'scientific' decisions, taken by designated experts and consultants, over the deliberative processes of organisational members, oriented towards an ISS that may not be reachable in practice, but which nevertheless serves as an ideal that can be striven towards, and is representative of different knowledge-forming practices. Colonisation results in even the objective rationality of such decisions being made subservient to the interests of money and power, which can distort them, both directly and indirectly. Less moneyed or powerful interests may simply be denied access to the spaces in which the results of their enquiries could be broadly disseminated and thus serve as a resource for others, within an organisation or outside it.

Education in a colonised environment also becomes an instrument, manipulated and wielded to help dominant interests meet goals. Curricula and key terms are controlled. What is defined as 'education'? Who is permitted to call themselves an 'educational provider'? What must one learn to be considered 'educated'? For example, Bailey et al (1998) review the Canadian national curriculum statement on 'scientific literacy'. It "is centered on science education for the development of skilled workers in the science and technology sector of Canada's economy", without mention that scientific literacy could potentially address questions of power and individual enlightenment. This is colonisation *par excellence*, Robins & Webster's "instrumental progressivism" (1987), a notion Whitworth (2010) considers deeply integrated into some, though not all, national IL policies. Bailey et al ask whose interests are served by such an educational *choice*, concluding that it is not the workers', but the gatekeepers', those with "coercive influence". From this perspective, educational practice works in contrast to certain professed targets, particularly the production of critical thinkers.

Indirectly, but just as significantly, colonisation erodes the right, and ability, of the mass to construct knowledge and ideas. It values not a broad polity, intersubjectively debating and reaching a consensus, but the objective, generic pronouncements of experts. Carr and Kemmis (1986, 70) write the following:

> (T)he fact that both pure and applied educational research demands considerable scientific expertise, implies that the only people competent to make decisions about educational policies and practices would be those who had acquired this expertise. Teachers, although they can be expected to adopt and implement educational decisions made on the basis of scientific knowledge, would not themselves participate in the decision-making process...

They note that this exclusionary perspective opens and sustains the theory-practice gap in education: a gap between those who make claims and those who test them. The suggestion can be applied to other fields, including librarianship (here see Julien and Williamson 2011).

To sum up, Habermas's theories describe how certain types of knowledge-forming practices (learning) are devalued compared with others. And because single-loop learning is oriented towards *preservation* and double-loop learning towards *transformation*, colonisation results in an increasing fixity of informational landscapes and the devaluing of local, indigenous, practice-based knowledge, in favour of those generic forms, which can be more easily manifested by information systems. It is not based around the scrutiny of validity claims, but rather its opposite – which means it is also a form of rationality conducive to the maintenance of hierarchy.

* * *

Habermas's work thus describes a shift within organisations to a more objective and hierarchical, and less intersubjective and consensual, set of practices and information exchanges. These can become embedded into sociotechnical systems and thus shape practice, and learning can be directly and indirectly controlled in order to keep these practices from being scrutinised and transformed by those affected by them. Yet within his framework, though the shaping of practice is real, it is not deterministic or totalitarian. Change and transformation – *de*colonising practice – can still occur, despite the pressures weighed against it (hierarchism, manipulation of the public sphere, and so on). What then is 'decolonising' activity, and what are the *necessary conditions* for the democratic transformation of practice to have a chance of success? What role does IL play?

Transformational potential remains present in Habermas's theories because, unlike in the earlier models of the Frankfurt School – but in common with Gramsci's notion of hegemony and counterhegemony – society is not perceived by him as monolithic. Colonisation produces contradictions and tensions that can be revealed by those affected by it, understandings which are *learning outcomes.* These can subsequently turn into further *learning opportunities* – challenges to validity claims and efforts to transform practice, which will sometimes be successful. Scott called these contradictions *hidden transcripts*: informational resources, including narratives, values, sources and texts, which reveal inconsistencies or hypocrisies within the discourse of the powerful (Scott 1990).

The lifeworld is comprised of a range of different *landscapes* rather than a single formation, and landscapes based more around hidden than dominant transcripts have been given various names, including "counterpublics" (Fraser 1992: also Fay 1975, 97; Clarke 1996, 109), a term which evokes the counterhegemonic nature of the spaces. These counterpublics – multiple and possibly competing – are arenas in which information is exchanged and authority distributed in ways that differ from dominant discourses. This does not make counterpublics innately democratic. A particular context might be undemocratic and anti-egalitarian, sometimes explicitly (Fraser 1992, 124): a street gang or neo-fascist organisation, for instance. But counterpublics also include communities of practice, networks, activist groups, learning communities and other spaces in which new ways of working, thinking, and communicating are explored. These enquiries create "laboratories of experience" in which "[n]ew problems and questions are posed. New answers are invented and tested, and reality is perceived and named in different ways" (Melucci 1989, 207). Around these new interpretations, communities actively develop collective identities (Melucci 1996, 50)[2]. Communicative spaces protected from repression are needed to bind these identities together and allow them to flourish, and transformational movements mobilise actors partly for the construction of such spaces (Melucci 1989, 220). Hamelink's vision of information literacy therefore explicitly requires *activism* to become reality.

Social movements – activist communities mobilised around political goals such as environmentalism, anti-capitalism, and religious fundamentalism – have been frequently studied, and represent a significant subset of society's counterpublics. These spaces are hands-on and practical, not abstract concepts. Within them, information is more often transmitted orally (or, now, through social media) and through lived embodied experience, rather than through the controlled, hegemonic narratives of the mainstream media, the analytical eye of the researcher, or formal assessments of profit, loss, effectiveness or other instrumental criteria. Anti-organisational forms are often driving the movement, and the whole process: "thrives on diversity, works best when embedded in its own locality and context and develops most creatively at the edges, the overlap points, the inbetween spaces – those spaces where different cultures meet..." (anonymous author in *Do or Die* #8, 3).

For Habermas, social movements are one example of "counterinstitutions" that develop "within the lifeworld in order to set limits to the inner dynamics of the economic and political- administrative action systems". They aim "to de-differentiate some parts of the formally organised domains of action, remove them from the clutches of the steering media, and return these 'liberated areas' to the action-coordinating method of reaching understanding" (Habermas 1987, 396). Politically active communities would therefore seem to be a key agent of decolonisation.

Yet at this point Habermas failed to explore – indeed, almost pulled back from – the implications of his theories. He is notably weak on descriptions of how, in real-life political situations, these counterpublics could give rise to genuine change, by transforming practice. Can so abstract a theory be applicable to the real world, shot through with distortions, inequities and power? As Blaug (1999, 54) says:

> (A) quite extraordinary number of books and articles on Habermasian theory end with a somewhat nebulous benediction to its empirical promise. Often, an increase in popular deliberation in the making of political decisions is called for, and general praise is inevitably heaped on the public sphere as the appropriate space for such deliberation.... No one feels able to bring him or herself to actually address the empirical problem of how the normative insights might be translated into institutional shape.

This problem is reflected in the title of Blaug's book (1999a): the difficulty in moving from *ideal* to *real*, recognising the possible contradiction in the idea of "design for democracy". The contradiction is manifested if democratic institutions or processes are foisted on a community without the agreement of that community. Yet if democracy *emerges* from the community, the contradiction is effaced, and Blaug says (1999a, xv) that such learning processes should at least expect *guidance* from critical democratic theory. For critical theory to be a "living force" it must be developed in association with contemporary issues and problems (Forester 1985).

Blaug points out that hierarchism, like other aspects of hegemony, usually works not by direct coercion and the oppression of alternatives. Practitioners advocating the spread of new values, organisational forms, and ways of thinking may be detained as subversives, or subject to disciplinary action or dismissal, but more frequently the operations of hegemony are less direct, with actors denied the methodological or conceptual tools to evaluate and learn about alternative ways of thinking and working. Nevertheless, learning *can* take place regardless of the controls placed on it, and: "In such a learning process, it may well be that Habermas's regulative ideal can help us 'train our eyes'..." (Blaug 1999a, 100).

Yet, like any other abstract and generic theory of human behaviour, only in a *context*, at the *moment of application* (*ibid*, 13), can the validity of the theory – thus, *the validity claim of the theorist* – be opened to scrutiny. Theoretical speculation "can never be a substitute for direct experience, for making mistakes, for seeing others do it well" (*ibid*, 100). This is, ultimately, the problem with Habermas: his lack of attention to actual, embodied human experience, and the *methods* by which new insights emerge and are validated. He pays insufficient attention to everyday communication and activity to give guidance and, where he tries, it is to a limited audience. The social movement is certainly an arena in which new, democratic possibilities are actively explored and one that, in early phases at least (*ibid*, 135*ff*), is characterised by great energy. But democratic moments, "laboratories of experience", arise whenever existing practices, habits, or routines are called into question, including between friends, parents and children, colleagues at work, doctors and patients, etc.

This perspective on democracy – the possibility of a distributed authority that is consented to, not hegemonically, but in an active and consensual way – is a necessary counterpoint to Foucault's view of power (1980) as embedded in everyday social interactions. The claim that democracy not only can be, but must be, a lived, embodied experience, invested in everyday practice, reclaims the notion from hierarchism. Hierarchism, the idea that authority should be concentrated rather than distributed, has promoted a political system that reduces the powerful notion of democracy to a remnant – the vote, and only for certain groups[3]. This system of political representation is called 'democracy', but it is quite a different beast from the lived and embodied experience. It is testament to the power of the word that it is retained for the impersonal and instrumental voting system, or as a synonym for 'Parliament' or 'Law'.

The role of "counterpublics", whether in their full form as social movements or simply as a space within a landscape in which practice is questioned, has been undermined in Habermas's work since *The Theory of Communicative Action*. "[A]s Habermas himself has admitted, by 1981 he had given up on the hope that the economy and the state could be 'transformed democratically from within'" (Hirschkop 2004, 52, via Habermas 1992, 444). By *Between Facts and Norms* (Habermas 1996), the public sphere and its component counterpublics became, for Habermas, not the source of political change but more a "sounding board for problems that must be processed by the political system" (Habermas 1996, 359; cited in Hirschkop 2004, 52; also Gardiner 2004, 29).

Yet though this may seem an "admission of defeat", "what the public sphere loses in terms of decision-making power it more than compensates for in terms of its ability to track the problems of capitalism down to their private lair" (Hirschkop 2004, 58). What Hirschkop means here (cf. Habermas 1996, 365) is that in the *personal spaces* of individuals and communities the impact of "systemic deficiencies" – exploitation, impoverishment, surveillance etc. – in late capitalist society are most clearly revealed. It is the lifeworld that "is uniquely suited to the demystifying of these problems in liberal capitalist societies" (Hirschkop 2004, 58), precisely because the lifeworld is defined by intersubjective exchanges that allow it to remain adaptable and responsive, rather than structured around instrumental solutions to problems that become reified ends-in-themselves. Thus, counterpublics and communities are better suited to double-loop learning. Without allowing for the questioning of the premises which underlie ways of thinking, and the systems based on them, transformation cannot occur (Hirschkop 2004, 60): "Through the crevices in discourse which allow one to 'open up' the discussion of life experiences, citizens are able to connect problems experienced in individual life histories to wider social structures."

Counterpublics, then, are the spaces in which the notion of *expertise* is reclaimed, and community members can discover they have something *valid* to say on issues that affect them, directly and indirectly. Counterpublics help assert the worth of forms of knowledge-making and self-expression that have been devalued by colonisation generally, and/or specifically repressed in particular contexts.

There is a risk of relativism once again. To say that political activism is legitimate simply because it exists and is structured in communicative ways would accommodate, say, the unstructured networks that are gang culture and Al-Qaeda. Both networks, in their own way, may have been

effective, but that does not mean they should be considered legitimate. From another perspective, the astrological "learning community" is one that is effective at producing and sharing information, and is built around particular media and linguistic conventions, despite having no scientific basis for its claims (Thompson 2008). Whatever radical IL is to become, it must be able to assess the values underlying communities like these, reveal and criticise them.

Revealing contradictions in a learning community is part of being *vigilant* over it. Blaug's discussion (1999a) casts democracy as a constantly-updating, dynamic environment that supports empowering, inclusive activities, not a system, an end-in-itself. A democratic environment would have to be constructed around the understanding that communicatively rational organisational forms, and discourses, constantly tend to decay. A supportive environment would slow this decay, by allowing for the continuous review and possible transformation of practice (Habermas 1993).

Blaug describes two reasons for this tendency towards decay. First, there are hegemonic pressures, which work to deny counterhegemonic, decolonising spaces the resources (financial, intellectual) from which they would benefit, and exploit those resources that do emerge from the space – matters already discussed above. Second, Blaug argues that to understand the pervasiveness of hierarchies, actors in social situations must understand the benefits they bring to decision-making.

Hierarchies are attractive for a reason. The limitations on the ideal of the ISS – the continuous exercising of double-loop learning – include time, cognitive biases, and the structures of language which result in differing interpretations (which is why some dissensus always has value: Lyotard 1984). Hierarchical decision making saves time and cognitive work, and as a result may even improve the prospects of truly democratic decision making. Abrahamsson (1993, 92–4) argues that hierarchy is useful for democracy, a rational installation as it allows decisions to not just be taken, but implemented. But the trade-offs involved show why we must be vigilant about hierarchies (Blaug 1999a), whether at state level, within organisations, or within communities.

The different epistemologies underlying each form of rationality use resources in different ways. In a communicatively-rational environment, knowledge is *formed* by keeping ideas foregrounded, and under scrutiny. Resources are needed to create the necessary supportive environment, including allowing practitioners time to undertake this work, and keeping debate and discussion flowing around the landscape. By its very